Finding My
Lost Life

The Fall to Addiction & Rise to Recovery

Based on a true story

BY JEREMY CROSS

ISBN: 978-1-0690680-3-3

Published by Jeremy Cross

Langley, British Columbia

First and foremost, I want to dedicate this book to my North Star, without you, none of this would have been possible. Thank you to my family's unconditional love and unbreakable bond. You all are the stars in my sky forever shining bright. When I faced death, it was all of you I wasn't ready to leave behind. You're the reason I kept holding on. I am grateful for rekindling my relationship with my higher power, you gave me purpose.

3

I can't believe I am actually in jail again. I can still remember how I felt when I first arrived here like it was yesterday. The iron gates of North Fraser Pretrial Centre loomed ahead, stark against the dull gray sky. As the transport van rattled over the gravel drive, I still remember staring out the small, barred window, my mind blank, yet heavy with the weight of my circumstances. This wasn't the first time coming here, but something about this time felt different. I felt exhausted. Colder. More final. The guards processed me with mechanical efficiency. Inmate 11209400 became my new identity again. I hated when they stripped, searched, and handed me a red jumpsuit, the fabric itching against my skin as I awkwardly had to get naked and change in the stale airless room. I have done this routine too many times, I thought. But this last time, the thought was tinged with something I was ready to acknowledge. Fear? Resignation? Both.

My cell is small and smells like sweat and regret and I feel like I'm suffocating as the air is filled with despair. The metal bunk beds that are built into the cement brick walls are so hard and uncomfortable. At least they supply a small television and basic cable. I would go insane without the TV, however the commercials are unbearable. The walls are decorated in pencil art full of tags and words from previous inmates. The unit consists of a main common area with five tables that each inmate gets while being served meals throughout the day. There is a weight room with tons of workout equipment and an outside yard with a basketball court and a fenced roof. There are around forty-five cells split up between 3 different levels, each having a balcony.

The toilet and sink in my cell are cold and metal. There is a tiny scratched out mirror. I can barely see my reflection or the red jumpsuit.

They "can" give you a red sweatshirt because it's quite cold in the jail. If you're lucky, they gave you one.

Depending on how crowded the jail is some people have to double bunk with another inmate. Something that everyone tries to avoid. I protested. I feel like I don't need to know someone else's daily bodily functions and I certainly don't need to be watched while I go to the bathroom. My cell door is solid steel with a little plexiglass window that overlooks the common area and the officers' podium desk that they sit behind and manage the unit from. They keep everyone locked up for the majority of the day, sometimes all day if the inmates are behaving badly, which is often. I can hear other inmates banging and yelling from their cells, screaming because they are experiencing withdrawals from drugs or alcohol and begging for medical attention. The guards have to do a walk-through every fifteen minutes. I watch them walk around and look into everyone's cell checking to make sure everyone is alive.

Luckily I have been in here for over five months now so I have stopped experiencing withdrawal symptoms. The loud unit door thunders and clanks open and I can see the guard marching in with someone new. I pray they stop before they get to my cell...I am on the third floor.

Slowly both of them walk up the first set of stairs, then the second, now they are walking toward my cell. I back away and close my eyes hoping maybe they are giving me a new neighbor or passing my cell. Then I hear the noise of keys threatening my space, it is about to be invaded. The door opens and a man enters. Fuck. We exchange pleasantries but I am hit with a wave of anxiety. He's kind of cute, his name is Tyler. A wiry man with a sharp jawline and covered in tattoos that snake up his neck. He had been in and out of prison his whole life and he is almost fifty.

Tyler asks me what I am in here for, which seems to be the main question when meeting other inmates. He is looking at me intensely as if he couldn't fathom how I found sobriety. There was something different about him- a restlessness, an energy that buzzed beneath his skin. For some reason I felt compelled to open up to him. Truly, I didn't want to get involved with anyone on the inside; prison friendships were dangerous, alliances even more so. Tyler was persistent, striking up conversations, asking questions. It wasn't long before I found myself opening up, my anxiety sunk down into the ground. He gave me a sense of comfort, perhaps I could finally really tell someone how I lost my life. So I began to tell him my story.

When I first got in here, the withdrawal was brutal. Every inch of my body ached, my muscles cramped and spasmed with a pain that tore through me like fire. I vomited until there was nothing left, my throat was raw and burning. The hours crawled by, each one a fresh hell, all I could do was lie on the cold concrete floor, my mind a twisted mess with regret and shame. I have been here before, but this time it was different. This time, there was no promise of relief on the other side, no escape plan. I felt trapped, and for the first time, I truly understood the depth of my addiction. It wasn't just the drugs that had me in chains; it was the trauma, the pain, the emptiness I had been running from for my entire life. I have been battling the disease of addiction and spiritual illness for the past seven years. My path was paved with challenges, self-discovery and profound transformation. For me, the decision to embrace sobriety marked the beginning of a journey that was as much about reclaiming my life as it was about rediscovering myself. It is a journey that requires courage, resilience, and a deep commitment to healing.

I began to recognize that sobriety is not just about abstaining from substances; it's about embracing a new way of living- one that is authentic, intentional and deeply rooted in self-care and personal growth. I have many reflections on the struggles and triumphs that come with recovery, tools that helped me build a life free from the grip of addiction, and encouragement to keep moving forward, even when the road gets tough. I am a testament to the strength and potential that exists within each of us. I hope not just to be an inspiration, but also to reassure anyone that struggles with addition that they are not alone.

The path to sobriety is challenging, but it is also incredibly rewarding. It is a journey that, with patience and perseverance, leads to a place of peace, fulfillment, and true freedom. I explicitly detail the events that took place when I was in active addiction - major traumas, many heart breaks, and many deceptions. Some of the content is quite disturbing. It is important to me that my story is complete and honest. I have spent the entire time while I was incarcerated at North Fraser Pretrial Centre writing a book on paper with a pen. I wrote about the validity of my true emotions and feelings in those exact moments of detox and withdrawal from fentanyl and crystal meth, as I wrote in the midst of it.

Addiction is when you have a strong physical or psychological need/urge to do or use something to bring about an altered state of mind or perception of reality. It's a dependence on a substance or activity even if you know it causes you harm. It can negatively impact your daily life and ruin your future. Addiction is a thief to the soul. It robbed me of my identity, my sense of self, my ability to sometimes love or be loved. My drug of choice was crystal meth and "Down", more commonly known as fentanyl or heroin. They were my destructive outlet to help mend what I knownow were oozing mental and emotional wounds from my relationships.

Only an addict can really understand the depths of what it means. When it comes to addiction, it's not only the addict who will be seeking recovery and forgiveness. If you're a loved one of an addict, my story hopefully can assist understanding the mindset of an addict. With that understanding it is easier to know what role you can or can't play in the addict's life. Many of my loved ones didn't know what happened to me. They often didn't know if I was safe or even alive and they were each affected differently. Many words were unsaid as countless time passed by. What no one knew was that I was in a life or death battle with addiction. Most do not understand how powerful and all consuming this is. I was a slave to the drug(s) and in total fear of the traumatic things I went through that go hand in hand with drug use. I was trapped in a cycle of self destruction, the more I tried to break free, the deeper I sank into the abyss. I became something and someone I didn't know or want to be. But addiction is not just about the substances-it's about the pain beneath them. For me, the drugs were a symptom of a much deeper wound, a wound that festered in the dark corners of my soul. I kept burying the trauma each time but it only kept growing stronger, feeding off my fear and shame until it became a force I could no longer ignore.

There aren't a set of rules or guidelines for someone going through the emotions of being a drug addict. I felt like I had nothing and no one. Completely isolated and riddled with guilt and shame so overbearing, I accepted that I wasn't getting out of this dark side of the world alive. It felt like a certainty. There's a moment in every addict's life when the facade shatters, when the illusion of control crumbles, and we are left staring at the wreckage of our life. For me, that moment came in the form of a near-fatal overdose. I remember waking up in a sterile hospital room, my body battered and broken, my mind a foggy and frightened mess. I had come face-to-face with death and for the first time in years, I felt something other than numbness - I felt fear finally when I entered into jail this time around. Fear that this is going to be my life; a revolving door in and out of jail.

The fear wasn't just about dying; it was about the realization that I had lost everything that mattered. I pushed away my family, destroyed friendships, and lost all sense of who I was. But in that moment of utter despair, something shifted. I knew that if I didn't change, if I didn't find a way to heal, I would lose myself completely. I had hit bottom, and there was nowhere left to go but up. I learned from my peer support worker there are two powerful pillars that are emulated; relatability and mutuality. In the spirit of these pillars, I share my story with you so that we can understand each other.

I have often found that the people not suffering from addiction (I call them "Muggles") have a simplistic understanding of what it means to be addicted. They call it a simple choice, or all that is needed is for the addict to ask for help. Addiction is so much bigger than that. These thoughts can belong to people who love you. For many, rather than seeing addiction as the way someone copes with their circumstance, they can't get past seeing it as a self-inflicted wound. And then, any hardship or horror that happens to an "addict" isn't seen the same way as it would if the same happened to a "muggle". It is too easy to see someone as an "addict" rather than a person. Being on drugs doesn't change the horror of that awful experience. Trauma comes in many forms and affects each person in different ways. For me, my trauma was compounded by horribly unthinkable situations that took place in my life during my time of addiction.

Relativity. Relatability. These words and idealisms are a secret ingredient to an addict's recovery. Many professionals or people in corrective job fields, such as clinical professionals, lack these qualities. What I went through can't be taught in a classroom. You won't find it in a text book. Unless you have personally lived and experienced what it's like to be an addict dealing with trauma, you simply won't understand and that makes it very difficult to be of service to an addict when coming from a purely academic background.

I felt like I was this high-tech broken spaceship so many people wanted to fix but they showed up with the instruction manual for something from Ikea. I was oozing in emotional and mental pain and everyone kept bringing band-aids for a bullet wound. It was a waste of time and the more complicated they made me seem, the worse I felt about myself and my addiction, which further exacerbated the place of hopelessness. I felt so misunderstood and with no way out.

The more fucked up I felt, the more I wanted to run. Making me feel more embarrassed which leads to wanting to use and need more drugs. Digging my hell-hole even deeper, everyday. Aiding an addict is like applying for a specialized trade where they require certain qualifications and certifications to be able to do the job. The "muggle" human simply can't relate making it impossible to understand. When I was in active addiction and clinical professionals in a suit tried to help me I'd tell them to "Fuck off". I felt there was no way they could understand me.

I feel like it's life and death here because addiction alters people and very often has the ability to kill. Addiction is a cold hearted bitch. It's narcissistic, cunning, and only cares about itself. It has the ability to change someone's life completely and make them into someone and something they never thought they could be. This is what happened to me. It made me capable of anything and willing to go through anything no matter how out of place I felt and I always felt out of place. The addiction part is just the tip of the iceberg and the symptoms and ramifications are everything you don't see as they're underwater from the outside looking in. It's like throwing a pebble into the water, the initial splash is just the beginning. All the ripples that follow are the damage and what I refer to as the symptoms of addiction.

My addiction, the drugs I used, was the fuel to the car as I drove through the shit storm that was my life. Everytime I refueled my car wore and tore more and more. Add to that the car needs premium and I kept filling it with regular gas.

While I was doing drugs, I thought I felt the power of being in control. I figured I was the one doing the drug, not the drug was doing me. That it was okay because I was driving the car. I did initially think drugs were my capital issue, later I found out that the drug was only the means to hide the real issues. The traumatic events in my life that took place before I started using played a huge role.

As I met other addicts, it became apparent that they all had a gateway drug, it is a very slippery slope. Some are "functioning addicts". This means they can be addicted to something and be able to hold a job, have their lives unaffected. Or so they think. They work Monday to Friday and party on the weekends. They are often referred to as "weekend warriors".

If you are an addict too, you're no different than me or any other addict. Don't think you have this addiction thing under control because you think your life is manageable. I get it. I used to think like that at the beginning. I never understood what someone meant when they would tell me, "it's a slippery slope".

Opening up my scars is extremely difficult for me. I've been running and hiding from my emotions and feelings since I was 10 years old, a part of that was my sexuality, but I didn't start using hard drugs as a warm blanket to wrap around my chilling trauma, until I was twenty-five. I'm someone who when looking in the mirror wants to like what he sees which is why I worked so hard on my physique and covered myself with meaningful tattoos.

Before I moved to downtown Vancouver I was born and raised in Langley. A rural farm setting with some smaller towns. I actually grew up on a farm. I grew up with my older sister, and shortly after my mom and my step dad married, they conceived my two younger brothers. As they got older and demanded more time and attention, that's when problems started to arise. My step dad was a cold, twisted man, he always treated me the worst. One of my fondest memories I have of him was when I woke up , I was in grade three, my older sister and I had received kittens for Christmas. It was a year later and my beautiful black cat, Stella, got run over . I remember running out to the back forest to see her and my step dad (former step dad), was walking back towards me with a shovel in his hand because he had buried her already. I remember bawling and running into his arms, it was the warmest thing he'd ever done.

I remember in highschool saying to my mom, "forget love, he doesn't even like me." I was always the one who got spanked, got things thrown at me, called names and always felt threatened. I was too scared to ever tell anyone or ask for help, my older sister could do no wrong, I could do no right. I hid my feelings well, I was on the honor roll and played high level hockey. I thought that was all I had to do to be invisible, so I tried. Even at school I'd get bullied and then come home to my step dad for more of the same, I didn't feel safe or accepted anywhere.

I lost my composure one time after he was more physical with me. I had to hide my sadness from my mom because if she was to find out that he was hurting me, she would be angry with him, thus, he would get more angry with me. But this one altercation I could not hide the tears and she became aware that he had been treating me badly. I couldn't hide the crying and she forced the reason for the tears out of me.

It felt like after this event they started having marriage issues and he became awful to her and me, but more frequently towards me. Resentment formed. I wasn't safe anymore…anywhere. I hated my life so hard, I wanted to take my life, I was so defeated. I had to get away.

My mom was devastated when I left for Kamloops to go to university but I had to escape. My step dad paid for my sister and me to return back home for Christmas to support my mother. I think he wanted to show that he finally wanted to listen to her by bringing back her two most valuable players in her life. A sign of love or support? I can't speak for him, I don't know what his intentions really were in doing this. I came back for winter break and I noticed my mom was different. She was in great spirits, looking fantastic, bubbly but she was fighting all the time with my step dad so it didn't make sense.

I knew something was up. When I came home for Christmas, my uncle (step dad's brother), who is usually quite shy and quiet, came over and my step dad was gone. He came into the house and asked me where my mom was. I said in her room, which was on the whole other side of the house, he had an envelope in his hand. He walked across the house to see her. I ran downstairs all the way to the unfinished basement which was directly under her room. I wanted to hear what was going on and make sure she was okay. I felt like something was wrong.

What I heard and will never repeat ,changed my life forever. I'll never forget the feeling. What their side of the family did to her and to us was soul crushing. As a result I began to see my mother in a different light, as a human, not just a mother. This is the first time I learned that my beloved mother, my hero, was also human. As bad as whatever mistake takes place, teaching your children that it's not about how hard you are pushed down, it's about how you pull yourself up. She taught me resilience and optimism. She taught me that it's okay to be human.

I went up to console her, she was in complete panic and shaken. This happened on December 23. My Christmas was spent rocking my mom to sleep, crying, setting up my little brother's santa presents and doing everything to give everyone else a stable day. The first year after that the Christmas magic was barren, my whole illusion was shattered.

When my step dad came back to the house it was WW3. He didn't have to be nice to me for my mom anymore, it seemed they were looking down the barrel of divorce. In a way, I was never given the chance to stop and heal. My life didn't seem to be sheltered at the time. I didn't have any sexual experiences before moving, nor did I yet know how corrupt and cruel the world could be. I did get a taste of cruelty when I went to Langley Secondary School for grades nine and ten. H.D. Stafford Secondary school joined L.S.S. while I was in grade ten, students from the two schools did not know each other. I was severely bullied. The boys used to spit on me in the hallway or hit my books out of my hands when they would walk past me. They shouted awful things at me. The popular girls from H.D.Stafford. were my friends, at this time. I was a closeted gay man which is why I connected easily with the girls and the guys didn't like that. It made me enemy number one and put a huge target on my back. I used to pretend to get math detention just so I could hide away during lunch but there was always a random guy that tried to fight me almost every day, huge crowds of people would be looking for me. I lived in constant anxiety and I was too embarrassed to tell anyone. All my close guy friends turned on me ,to join the cause, so they could fit in. I used to work at Canadian Tire and I would try to always take the bus early so that I could avoid the after school crowd so that I didn't get beaten up. I didn't go to any school functions because I was too afraid and I had to quit the hockey academy because there wasn't enough teacher supervision and "the boys" would always "hate" on me. It was torture, I hadn't done anything to deserve this kind of treatment. I finally left LSS and went back to D.W. Poppy, a school I attended previously, for my senior years and was popular again. Ever since that day I used my popularity for good, I stood up for and supported those who were being bullied.

Getting my driver's license when I was 16 gave me a little more freedom. I got a girlfriend and I was captain of the hockey team. The assistant captain was a guy named Cole. We became best friends, being so close, something more started, something that solidified what I feared. I liked how a boy made me feel. I liked what my girlfriend made me feel as well but not as much. We had a secret love affair that no one knew about. We went to the same highschool for grade 11 and 12 at D.W.Poppy.

Being that I was gay and virgin to it all, when Cole and I began, I didn't know what to think of it, I just knew I loved him. We did everything together. Over a year went by, then my girlfriend cheated on me so I was single.. Rumors went around that Cole and I may be more than best friends which caused him to spook and become angry with me. It was like he hated me for making him feel some sort of way. He tried fighting me, he hit the mirrors off my car in the school parking lot, he tormented me, threatened me in all sorts of different ways. It was gut wrenching. I was stunned. I couldn't bring myself to hate him back, simply because I didn't. I looked at a way to explain why he reacted so negatively.

Cole has many brothers, for him, being gay would be a tragedy so he turned on me. I was devastated, heart broken, confused, alone. Because I was closeted and I didn't want to "out him", I suffered alone. To be honest, call it naive, I didn't know what being in the closet was at the time either, I hadn't questioned my sexuality at all growing up. I was just taught to like girls as that was the social norm, and I did have crushes on girls in elementary school. I hadn't given any thought to looking at a boy as more than a friend, until Cole. Once it happened, I started to educate myself on what it means to be gay. I experimented with guys to see if what I was feeling was true. Once I had a taste of the feeling I got from a man, I remember thinking if this is wrong, then I don't want to be right.

I lost my girlfriend and Cole within the same month, I was shattered. I couldn't tell anyone. This all happened in my senior year of highschool. It was a difficult time, this was the first time I could physically feel my heart break. A part of me thought that this was my punishment for being unfaithful to my girlfriend with Cole. I never wanted any other girl, I loved her whole heartedly, but not in the same way that I loved Cole. I wasn't doing it to be deceitful, it wasn't even premeditated. It just formed, the electricity between us just struck us both and we didn't even really acknowledge what was happening. Cole became my first form of abuse, unique in the way that it was the first person that I loved that attacked my heart. The first person that made my mind and my heart confuse each other.

My older sister moved to the island, leaving me alone in the house with my two very much younger brothers. Another loss that made my life difficult to understand.

I now felt like there was a dragon living inside me that really wanted to break free sexually, so finally owning that I was gay heightened those feelings. Coming out of the closet for me was nerve racking. My family was extremely supportive, as were my closest friends, it's not like I suddenly changed my character or demeanor. I did feel the weight of the rainbow, being that I now belonged in the gay category and this bothered me.

I think I just like people. After coming out, I did fall in love with other women. The way I look at it is, if there was my perfect ideal man and woman in front of me, I would without a doubt choose the man, however I would be fine with the woman as well. Either way the selection pool in Langley is very slim. I suffered from depression and anxiety and being so young I didn't know where to find resources or how to ask for help. I felt like I was isolated. I was ill equipped to handle and deal with everything going on in my life. My parents didn't prepare me for what would possibly happen next and what the drug world entailed, but how could they as they've never been a part of it.

It was the men I dated who would play a paramount role in my story. I don't blame them, I know that I am ultimately responsible for my own behavior, but I must also recognize the role they played. (For privacy and confidentiality reasons I am going to sub out their real names with pseudonyms as I don't want my words to embarrass or hurt anyone. I don't hold any hatred or resentment towards them. The intention of sharing my story isn't to be malicious, I want to share my story to bring awareness to many different things for many different reasons. I understand that everyone has their version of the story and I have to be okay with the fact that they may conflict with mine, all I can do is be myself and hold my head up high with honesty and integrity. These men may still be very deep in their battle with addiction and I, better than anyone, understand what it's like to become someone very different. I can't condemn them for who they were to me and what they did to me. Drugs don't excuse their actions but I at least can understand it. I would like to think that if they weren't on drugs, their treatment of me would have been a lot different.

I did experiment with club drugs as a young man here and there with close friends from Langley, but nothing very serious, nor was I addicted to the drugs I used. When I say club drugs, I mean cocaine and MDMA. I never was a part of the Vancouver gay scene until I moved down there because I would never leave my girlfriends that I came to the club with for a man, we always stayed together.

My dream was always to live right in downtown Vancouver in a highrise. I wanted to look out my window and be surrounded by other highrises. Glass everywhere covered in city lights with the white noise of city life surrounding me. I had to be downtown, I didn't want to be in Langley. There aren't any gays there especially compared to the gay scene downtown and I like the hustle and bustle, the energy, and the possibility of meeting someone else who loves the color and energy.

I met Luke online. He was a man who was in AA and living a healthy and sober life, I liked that about him. I didn't know anything about AA yet, it intrigued me. I had no idea at the time that he would be the person to change the entire course of my future, and change the way my heart beats. We both had full time jobs when we met. He worked as a contractor downtown Vancouver and I worked at a company called Talius as the chief of operations in Coquitlam. It was a company that did the manufacturing and installation of roll shutters and blinds. They are meant to be used as protection for store fronts. The fancy blinds were generally bought by the rich to block the sun in their homes. We moved in together shortly after meeting, I was so attracted to him.

We went to the gym everyday, ate healthy, and lived 5 minutes from the downtown core. I owned a pearl white, fully paid off, $40,000, 2015 Kia Optima Hybrid. I picked him up every day after work. We shared a place together with two other boys in a split level apartment on Tisdal Street.

I went as a supporter to his AA meetings, little did I know he had a secret, something I wasn't aware of. Luke proposed to me after dating for a year on the beach in downtown Vancouver. Luke's mother died young and he had battled with addiction since he was a teen . He was a hyper sexual man and taught me it's okay to embrace sexual expression. I didn't know how much I loved it. He didn't have any money so I bought my own ring but he insisted on being the one to propose.

He was super controlling and made me exercise my people pleasing side our entire relationship. It was his way or no way. I thought he was only going to AA for the addiction with alcohol. I had no idea what I was getting myself into and the baggage he truly carried. For better or for worse…I love hard which made me hang on so tightly even when I realized our relationship was abusive. I think being a product of divorce played a huge role in my behavior and outlook on my relationships.

I love my parents and am close to them, making it easier to be around them and respect them. I didn't know how much damage it had done. When I suddenly had a step parent besides the two of them and that they didn't stand together anymore, I grew resentful towards the idea of separation. I never felt like I had my amazing dynamic duo parents again.

My dad dated different women, none were really bad, they just weren't my mom. My mom married a man who ended up being abusive to me. Very abusive. Something I hid from everyone for years growing up, I was in constant fear. After years of abuse, I felt he certainly lost the right to be called my Dad. Looking back, I think subconsciously I hated that my parents weren't together. I can't imagine what my life would be like if they stayed together. To have them together would have been incredible because they are good at being a Mom and Dad.

I wouldn't trade my four younger half-siblings for anything though. But this impacted my willingness to make my relationships work - even if loving them was destroying me in the process. I would set myself on fire to keep others warm even when I knew it was time to leave or break things off. I didn't act on it.

Maybe this is a deep ripple effect of divorce, being a child of one when I was so young. I have memories of my dad dropping me off back at my mom's house after spending the weekend with him (that was their court ordered set up, my sister and I would go to his house every second weekend). I remember bawling my eyes out, I was five, watching him as he drove away, from my bedroom window, out of the cul-de-sac. My mom tried comforting me, a couple minutes later, my dad appeared in my doorway to try and defuse this manic episode. I didn't know how scared I was to "divorce" my partners even after suffering abuse because it was an emotional wound that was never brought to the surface. I had such huge resentment towards the fact that two of my favorite humans couldn't stay together and it broke me internally. So I did everything in my power to not break away from my partners because I was so scared of repeating and experiencing my parents' relationship and all the heartbreak that it had caused.

I had a problem or fear, with breaking things off, trying to do anything to make it work. I am super territorial and love the idea of someone thinking and loving the idea that I'm theirs and they are mine. This is why I never believed in cheating and why being cheated on was crippling for me.

Luke changed, he decided he wanted a polyamorous relationship which is the practice of, or desire for, romantic relationships with more than one partner at the same time with the informed consent of all partners involved. He instigated this some time after we were already engaged. It didn't seem fair that his life proposal towards me was in a monogamous fashion and then suddenly he changed the dynamics. I was heartbroken. I didn't want to feel like I wasn't enough, or unworthy of being good enough for a man. The thought of him wanting more than I could offer hurt me so deeply. I don't fault him on this, he is of course entitled to live whatever life he desires, but it still hurts. Especially because other men had desired just me, but the person I picked wanted more. He was the first very attractive man that loved me and we had ,what I thought, was a real grown up relationship. I loved him so much. I tried to have threesomes with him, with guidelines in place, such as being a package deal and he made it perfectly clear that if I didn't participate he couldn't be with me.

It started to feel like we were always in a competition. Someone would always be more attracted to one person and being that I was "new meat" in the gay scene and because of how I looked, especially my tattoos, I was getting more attention than Luke. I felt like I was his "shiny toy". He took me for granted. He got bored, so he would toss me aside, he wanted to taste

other things but when he saw how much attention I was getting and how many men wanted to be with me, his "toy", he would clam up and not want to share me with them.

The situation worked to my advantage because sharing Luke was killing me. I hated it. I would want to break whoever the third party joining us was. I tried everything. I almost destroyed myself doing it. When we would engage in a threesome, I wouldn't be able to get excited because when the other person would touch him, I'd get angry.

One of the times I took injectable viagra because oral pills weren't strong enough for me to be aroused, I was not into the idea of sharing him. It gave me a weapon for a very unsafe amount of time. I was rushed to St. Paul's Hospital Emergency because it was so painful and shouldn't have lasted that long. The nurses had to inject an I.V. into the side of my shaft in order to bleed the blood out manually. I almost lost the ability to have natural erections if they didn't get the blood out quickly enough. They injected six long needles around the shaft to numb it for the installation of the I.V. It was one of the most painful things I've ever had to endure. When they were operating on me, I held Luke's hand and squeezed so hard that I nearly broke it.

Even though I hated this forced dynamic I tried everything in my power to make our relationship work. The hospital incident scared Luke from wanting to open up our relationship because I was hurt and he felt responsible. The guilt didn't last long; he eventually said he needed to continue to have an open relationship and I could either stay or go. It put me in a very uncomfortable position. As much as it killed me, I stayed because I didn't want to lose my Vancouver lifestyle. I knew we were done and even though I kept the ring on my finger, he wasn't the one I was going to marry. Even though marriage was no longer an option our "relationship" continued, but things got worse.

Luke relapsed to crystal meth. This was the secret he had hidden from me, I didn't know he had a history with hard drugs. He had introduced me to GHB, a gateway drug, making sex fantastic and I assumed that this was as far as it would go. I didn't know the fire that we were sparking.

Crystal meth and sex is a monster on its own and has a major role in the downtown gay scene. You either shoot or smoke crystal meth and some mix it with water and put it in their bowel which is called "hooping". It's euphoric when you shoot it in the vein. It's like nothing I'd ever experienced and it makes sex unbelievable.

I never thought I'd ever get involved with these drugs, I'd seen all the high school specials on drugs. I thought meth heads were homeless people picking their own skin on the street; the scum of the earth. Never did I think the person I loved would be telling me "it's okay" and hand me the pipe. It's really "mind fucking" when the person you love is telling you something is okay when you know it's not. I watched the effect that the drug had on him, it changed his demeanor.

He was not a functioning addict, once the drug took hold of him, everything we had built started to decay. He got fired from his beloved job as a contractor. He texted me while I was working at Talius and told me he was going to kill himself. I knew he was high when he texted me and I rushed home immediately. It was unlike Luke to talk like this. I knew that if he was high, he would want sex and I was scared he would cheat on me so I felt I couldn't go to work and I didn't want to leave him alone.

Now I knew this should have been the moment I got the fuck out, but I refused to leave him. I was getting so much sexual attention from him and the dragon within me was finally getting released. I felt so alive and desired, which had taken a hit when he originally declared he wanted more men, so him wanting me again "all the time" was euphoric. I couldn't help it.

Everything feeling so incredible and new was the effect the drug had on me, but it came with a price. I was let go from my job. We had bills to pay and no money coming in so Luke pitched the idea for us to escort. Luke knew how to do escort because he had done it before he met me to support his drug habit in the past. I had always thought people doing drugs weren't successful or couldn't be. Crystal meth and GHB were the two most common drugs associated with sexual behavior while we were on a gay escort on "leolist" online, and "grindr" app. and many other dating apps, we used every day to connect with successful professionals. They would hire us for varying amounts of time then return to their families. I struggled with this whole thing from the beginning. It felt unnatural. I am so against the idea of selling my body for money or sharing my body with someone I wasn't attracted to.

I was stunned. In my right mind I would never participate in doing something like this, escorting, however drugs and sex at this level alter minds. I agreed to try duo escorting and we made good money. I had accepted the fact I was leaving him eventually so I was suddenly fine with sharing him. I knew he wasn't the one, so I learnt about the sex trade from him and the role it played in the dark side of the world.

It felt very wrong to stay with someone I knew I didn't love, and even disliked, but I stayed physically planted. On a deeper level, it felt like I was deceiving my own soul.

It really screwed me up mentally because I had these very successful doctors and lawyers hiring me as an escort; buying my time for a very high price. I was still using drugs and they were requesting to party on drugs with us, PNP, ?using my expertise to buy and help them either smoke or inject crystal meth.

We posted nude photos on different gay apps and became really popular. We were able to pull this lifestyle off for a short amount of time. People started to ask to hire us separately which was the start to our interesting dynamic demise. I was desired and did most of the work but he controlled me and the money. When his physical health started to deteriorate (he couldn't keep his body healthy or his appearance on point) it made him less desirable for hire. I was still in tiptop shape. When I received the attention, he got abusive and the jealousy set in.

When he started treating me like "shit" and being more outwardly abusive, I realized I needed to make a change. He was extremely controlling in our separation. When we had to leave Tisdal Street, I found a one bedroom apartment on Burnaby Street in downtown Vancouver. There were a few weeks during the transition period where we would have been homeless so one of our clients let us stay in his extra room in his penthouse on Cambie Street. He was a super nice man, a very successful dentist who took a liking to us when we were escorting together. However, little did I know this was going to push me even deeper towards the corrupt, dark side of the world. We all shot up crystal meth, and at this point Luke was in one of the phases where he closed up our relationship not wanting to share his toy (me) which drove this client mad.

One night, after staying up for too many consecutive days, the client had a mental snap. Luke and I were sleeping with the door closed and Luke had a night terror which woke me up. Our client came running in asking if everything was okay. I calmed Luke down and the client went into the kitchen to get Luke a glass of water, which was just beside our room. I remember hearing something weird, so I looked at the wall outside of our room where there was a large picture hanging. In the glass reflection I could see into the kitchen and the client was glaring at us. It was like something demonic came over him. I turned around to give Luke a "what the fuck" look, Luke screamed and I turned around. The client came running in the room, before I could respond he lunged at me, grabbing my tank top, yanking me close towering over me. I struggled and tried to break free but he was too strong. Panic surged through me as I realized I was outmatched. He tossed me aside and lunged at Luke. He screamed bloody murder so I turned around and gave him a swift kick in the guy's midsection and he grunted in pain, this loosened his grip on Luke, just enough so he could wiggle free. I didn't hesitate, I grabbed him by the back of his shirt, reefed him out through the door and then slammed and locked it shut.

He was swearing and screaming. It was insane. He went into the kitchen and got a knife and tried to break open the door. We were scared for our lives.

Eventually Luke called the police and they found the client on the 5th floor which was weird, because you have to have key fobs to get anywhere in the building and we weren't on that floor. Apparently he was unconscious when the police found him. We rushed to the hospital where he was taken. The police were acting strange when we arrived. They asked for our version of the story but were standoffish with Luke and me.

We returned to the penthouse and waited for his release. On his return, he acted calm and the police came to check on us. When they arrived, our client handed the police an envelope full of cash. Luke and I were then instructed to leave and find a new place, no charges were made and the attack was minimalized.

It was bizarre. We were the victims, unprovoked, and this didn't seem like proper protocol for the police. Luke and I were stunned and confused with the whole situation. For me this was a sneak peak of the corruption in the world, something I was never exposed to in my earlier years. It's amazing how people of different powers and societal positions are treated by law enforcement and the power money has. If Luke or I had done what our client did, we would have been locked in jail and charged with attempted murder or assault.

Luckily, my mom helped us financially to acquire the new place on Burnaby Street or we would have been homeless. In my eyes, our new place should have been more mine than his, but I never technically enforced this until we had a huge blow out. I finally found the courage to be independent so Luke started to lash out at me because I found my backbone. He took my car and crashed it in the back alley behind our apartment. When I went out back to retrieve my car, I came back to him throwing my clothes out the window for everyone to see. He stole our escort client list and emails which were very valuable. I had created and organized our company. I was still heartbroken from what Luke had done to me so when I should have been angry, I was still sad. He was my first love which made me weak. He also was, at this point, considered a part of my family, my mom paid for him to come to Mexico with us for Christmas so this made the separation a much bigger deal than just a simple breakup.

I was so disappointed. From the outside looking in, we appeared to be a happy power couple, but looks can be deceiving. I felt like I was sitting on a chair inside a burning building and looking around and acting like everything was okay. Positivity became a stranger and sex became emotionless.

I betrayed love, love betrayed me. I feel I was forced to love wrong. My feelings and emotions were never considered with Luke, I was always walking on eggshells around him. This was my first interaction with a narcissist, I just didn't know what that really was at the time.

My landlord owned two rental properties and he allowed Luke take me off the rental contract unlawfully by forging my signature, which made it fraudulent. Luke had found a random guy to move in, to take my place, without my consent and went to our landlord and verbally said I was okay with it, so he signed my rights away, without me even being present. He put in this other person's name where mine was on the contract. I threatened the landlord to go public with what had happened, because I didn't agree to taking me off of the contract until I had secured another place. To keep me from going public, the landlord allowed me to move in at a lower rate into the other rental on Barclay Street in downtown Vancouver. Luke kept all the furniture, I was left with nothing. So I took some of the little things that he allowed me to keep and moved there by myself. I had to move out of my Burnaby Street apartment, I allowed him to keep the place because I couldn't deal with what had happened causing so much stress.

I restarted my escorting market alone and let him have the previous contact list because of his extreme spite and vindictiveness I didn't have the capacity to cope with all the devastation, I had no time to digest anything he was making me deal with or any time to even think because everything was moving too fast.

Despite the hurt caused by Luke and how he went about closing this last chapter in our lives, I was finally excited. All new things for an all new me. I felt like my new apartment on Barclay Street was perfect. A cheap studio apartment right in the middle of "Gayville" which was perfect for escorting since that was my only source of income.

I was super successful. I had very nice things, a well furnished apartment and to top it off, was very popular. I had put aside $20,000 in my safe after living there for only a couple of weeks from solo escorting.

I was exposed to many different, extremely fucked up sexual things, during my encounters with all different kinds of people. I thought, I finally felt happy, with all my current successes and feeling like I looked the best I ever looked. Anyone that saw me would have thought that I was so happy and healthy, but in turn, I was in the worst condition I had ever been. Happiness was an illusion. The more I objectified myself the more drugs I needed to cope and the deeper I got with addiction. It felt right on a general surface level because I physically looked good, I was making lots of money and made so many connections, especially putting myself out there and meeting other gay escorts doing the same things I was. I continued to judge myself because it felt wrong to share my body with strangers for money and I still needed "meth" to be able to accept this life I was living.

There was something fascinating about the feeling that being an escort gave me. I had a new respect for the sex trade. The sexual exposure made me feel alive, it gave me an escape from a me that I wasn't fully happy with before. It actually helped my self confidence. I was often stunned to find out what sexual fantasies other people had. Some men just wanted to lick the bottom of my shoe, some wanted to watch me go to the bathroom - odd to me. I was surprised to find that some just wanted to talk, be alone with me, naked, but just talk. I set my restrictions and boundaries with what I offered. It really surprised me to find that a lot of the men didn't actually want to have sex, in fact I barely had to. I was different then other escorts though and I was told that all the time because I actually liked to converse and get to know my clients. It helped to form mini relationships with them and they started to actually care about and look after me. I was a whole different package, it wasn't just about the money, I also was able to counsel a lot of them and they continued to come to me for help, men of all different ages and walks of life. I think because of this, I thought I was happy, I was getting a fulfillment of sorts.

The business activated a very private and tender human connection. It felt good that another human chose me to share themselves with me, it stroked more than just my delicate ego. I was still damaged goods at this point, heartbroken and very mentally mixed up. Seeing Luke on gay hookup sites knowing that he was having sex with random people without me, still took the air out of my lungs, felt like I was being kicked in the balls, it was a wound that had not yet healed.

Yet, I was the talk of the town, one of the more successful and known among the sex trade world. Still very much a virgin to it though, I was winging it most of the time but I conducted myself very professionally. What I didn't know was that having nice things made me a target to many and caught the attention of some of the most devious men in Vancouver. I was sought out by a famous fraudster which altered the course of my life forever. I was unaware that my life was about to change for the worse. When I met him, I had no idea what fraud was, or being someone's mark.

Being someone's mark is a terrible thing and it means that you are prey and have been carefully chosen by an individual with an evil agenda. You are disposable. It's a game that involves serious sadistic deception. The hunter is someone using every manipulative weapon possible; mentally, verbally and physically. These people like to gaslight. It is the highest form of mental manipulation that makes you question your own reality and insanity. This person has a secret agenda and intention to take a person over. They look at someone as a dollar sign…an object. Tricking an innocent and uneducated person by doing whatever means necessary, like getting you to fall in love with them so they can control everything about you.

I didn't know this fraudster was on Canada's "Most Wanted" for major fraud charges. He introduced me to another fraudster named Kyle. I wasn't particularly attracted to him at first, I didn't know what Kyle was or wasn't into. He saw that I would be the perfect mark as I knew nothing about anything in his world..

At the beginning Kyle was the perfect gentleman. He held the door open for me and considered me this beautiful trophy that he obtained. He fooled me so well with his evil genius and perfectly orchestrated plan to corrupt me. I see that now, but at the time I was completely blinded.

In this dark world of crime, everyone knows everyone, so nobody wanted to help me or get involved because they didn't want to capture Kyle's attention. He was fixated on me which I, at the time, felt flattered. He controlled me; he had my heart. He carefully twisted and turned my reality. He was such a master craftsman that I was a fool for him.

Kyle eventually did heroin and fentanyl (the same family). He became a monster on it. It is so powerful, when he was "Down sick", he would sell his own mother to get his fix. He did let his walls down with me and told me he loved me and at first I thought we were very much in love. It was like he was fighting himself, he wasn't used to unconditional love. We were very into each other but when heroin took hold of him, everything started to change. I didn't realize the minute he did, a third person entered our relationship, the drug, and I wasn't its equal. Heroin trumps all other drugs, it trumps all other things. It stole him from me, I just didn't know it. As a result of Kyle's addiction and my feelings for Kyle, I was pulled into another life.

Kyle exposed me to tons of different crimes: back alley deals, stealing, shoplifting, breaking into vehicles, lobbies, mail theft, car theft, credit card fraud, bank fraud, insurance and property fraud and those are just some. When we started dating, we both were not allowed to escort so we needed to find a way to make money to support our lifestyles. At first, he kept this part of his world private from me, I knew nothing about crime. I could see how broken he was, he was so tender with me when he wanted to be. It was quite masterful and super seditious. He was a pro at picking and choosing his moments of when to show great love towards me and to masquerade hate.

He would disappear for hours and days, I didn't know what he was up to. I didn't know what this type of behavior meant. He didn't have his own place or car, I was never made aware of his living situation which is why he was always at my condo. I didn't do heroin and I still had money saved away for rent and what not, he never asked me to use it to supply his drug of choice, at first. When we would buy crystal meth for us both, the dealer would just throw in some heroin for him, I didn't know what the money was being used for, I just naively allowed him to do the transactions because it was his dealers. He hid it from me by putting heroin only in his pipe and mixed it with crystal. But I started to see that his high was very different from mine. I thought he was something I could fix because I could tell he, in his own way, was broken. I thought that he was just robbed of what true love should look like and be like. I was easily manipulated by him, but finally an event that took place finally pulled the blinders away.

Kyle and a bunch of guys did a big score involving credit card fraud somewhere in Vancouver away from me, because at this time, he still kept me isolated and very uneducated, still unaware of what his true intentions were with me and how he really felt about me and what he was really doing when I wasn't around.

He never split the proceeds of the score with the other men… I later found out. These guys figured the only thing valuable he had was me. Hitting me meant hitting him where it hurts. I was dating Kyle, so I didn't escort anymore. These three men came to my home, Kyle had given my address and they figured I was bought and paid for because Kyle owed them from not splitting the money from the deal they all did together. Apparently the amount owed was the time they had with me.

There was a knock on my door, I opened it, I thought nothing of it. The three men standing in the doorway fell silent as I opened the door, I could feel their eyes on me. They walked in slowly and they all stared at me. I had no idea who they were. At first I was kind and said, "Hi, can I help you?". All of them were big men, they didn't answer but just kept walking towards me, not breaking eye contact. My smile was wiped off because I could tell something wasn't right. A chill creeped down my spine, my heart sank. The first thought was they were here to rob or hurt me. These men clearly believed they had power over me by the way they just entered and there was a grim energy to them. My pulse quickened, a knot formed in my stomach. The last one through the door closed it behind him. I tried to keep calm, my heart was pounding, I tried to look around for something I could use as a weapon but I didn't want to break eye contact, just in case. The biggest one said as he circled me, "your boyfriend owes us a debt, so we've come to collect it from you", their faces filled with a mixture of amusement and something much darker. Fear got a grip on me, my mind raced, searching for a way out but I was surrounded. Two of them lunged at me and grabbed each of my arms to hold me down and forced me onto the bed. The third one began to take his pants off, it wasn't a battle that I was going to win which was clear to me when I screamed for help but they covered my mouth, my cries were swallowed by the night. It was extremely forceful. I was shocked and pierced with confusion. It felt wrong, everything was wrong. All my faculties were taken over, I couldn't even breathe, I was numb, I couldn't believe that I, a man, was getting raped. I fought with everything I had, my heart pounding in my ears, but they were stronger, they were many. The fear and adrenaline made my whole body shake as I tried to resist, but it felt like drowning, like fighting against a tide too powerful to overcome.

"Please! Stop!" I cried, but my words fell on deaf ears. The men laughed as they continued to restrain me, their grip tightening, their intentions clear. Every fiber of my being screamed in protest, but they didn't care. To them, I was a plaything, a momentary amusement in the dark. The one covering my mouth was also covering my nose, making it impossible to breathe if I protested, so to be able to actually breathe I had to stop resisting. As my strength retreated, I surrendered. I laid there lifeless. Each had their way with me, two would hold me down while the other did his thing, and they rotated. I closed my eyes and just let the panic overtake me. All I could do was wait for it to be over. I heard the door slam shut. I opened my eyes, I collapsed onto the ground off the bed, naked, shaking and trembling with anxiety. The nightmare had finally ended. I had survived but the memory of that night would stay with me forever.

I can still remember the dark eyes of these men. Angry... Animals. I laid there naked and terrified. Violated. Horrified. The worst part was shortly after they finally left, Kyle came over and acted like it didn't happen. Emotionless. I had marks all over my body, my place was a mess from my attempt to fight them off. My place was always spotless and he knew what had happened but still played stupid and didn't care about what I had just gone through and knowing it was his doing. He wasn't phased. My trauma went unanswered and unvalidated. My heart was so betrayed, I thought I experienced shock before but this was on a whole other level.

You would have thought that I would have known it was time to cut him off or make a change but I was under his spell. However this did taint our relationship because there was no excuse for him not to care. Even on a human level, not having compassion or empathy for someone that went through this was strange and hurtful. I don't know why he didn't care. Many friends tried to convince me that he was playing me but he made himself my hero by the way he was gaslighting me, and suddenly attraction was created and any doubts I had disappeared.

He had me tweaking on drugs, which was daily, altering my reality impeccably. He knew what amount of drugs to give me, how to keep me up for days, when to give me certain kinds of attention. He used and abused me.

I really had no idea he had a history with the Vancouver Police Department for the decade before he met me and they were on his tail. I hadn't really ever met a criminal before this so I didn't know the characteristics of one. I didn't know what it was to be a criminal. I've never had any issues with the law, so he started putting me in all the wrong places at all the right evil times and just by being with Kyle, it put a target on my back. He was using my identity to commit fraud, using me as a shield with the police and I was just that silly fool madly in love with a con artist. My heart got me in so much trouble. I was the perfect mark.

Kyle stripped me of everything I owned and everything I had. All my bank accounts, my credit, stole my identity and so much more. He went into ICBC and put his actual photo on my driver's license so he was able to commit a crime and get caught, in my name, which issued warrants that I didn't know about, getting me arrested. It was a disaster.

He would often lie about going somewhere just so that he could cheat on me. He told me he was going to the clinic to get his methadone one time and the way he just suddenly disappeared and didn't tell me where he was going sparked suspicion. I called the methadone clinic and they told me that he wasn't there. I called his phone and he said he went to his family doctor instead of the methadone doctor which I thought was odd. I called his family doctor, they said they hadn't seen him for months.

I sat on the front steps to my condo waiting, preparing. As soon as he arrived, I asked for his phone assertively (which I never was). He fought with me. Every time he looked down I yelled because I didn't want him to get any time to erase anything and there shouldn't have been anything to hide. He had looked at my phone all the time. I didn't care.

Grindr had been downloaded, which was already cheating in my eyes to start. Then I read the chats and found out he hooked up with a guy. I couldn't move, it was as if my body had frozen in place, my mind refusing to process what my eyes were seeing. The weight of betrayal settled over me like a heavy blanket, suffocating and inescapable. I always imagined betrayal would feel like a sharp knife to the heart, a sudden and violent pain. But this…this was worse. It was a slow, creeping numbness that spread through me, chilling my blood and turning my thoughts into ice.

I thought about all the times that he had told me he loved me, the way he smiled at me, the way we had made plans for our future and now it felt like a cruel joke. I wondered how long he had been lying to me, how many times he had cheated on me with other men while I was blissfully unaware. There was a hollow ache in my chest, a deep sense of loss that went beyond the betrayal. It was the loss of everything I thought I knew, the loss of the man I loved, and the life we were building together. I felt like a fool, like I had been living in a dream while the real world crumbled around me. Everything was blurred as tears filled my eyes. I had always been strong, the one who kept it together when things got tough. But now, I felt like a broken vase shattered into a thousand pieces, too small and too fragile to ever be put back together.

I dropped to the ground in front of Kyle, my breath coming in ragging gasps. I pressed my hands against my face trying to cover it, trying to hold back the sobs that threatened to break free. But they came anyway, wracking my body with a pain that felt like it would never end. In that moment, I realized that betrayal wasn't just about the act itself. It was about the trust that had been shattered, the love that had been stolen. It was about the loneliness that settled into my bones, the feeling that I would never be whole again. I know I will remember this moment when I try to open my heart again.

He would use my things without my consent, throwing my car keys down from my apartment window to someone else so they could use my car with my plates and commit crimes while Kyle would keep me occupied, so I wouldn't realize.

I would get in my car some mornings and there would be random mail and my seat was in a different position, Kyle wouldn't say anything. I knew, but I didn't know, I just couldn't fathom that someone would do that to a person they say they love. When I started to get more involved ,because he couldn't hide the devious part of his life from me any longer, we would do scores with other people. I voiced my opinion which was sometimes better, he would tell me to shut up and that they already had it covered. I was useless in his eyes.

He didn't have a place or car and had no money. He had nothing to offer me but somehow he was in control of everything. I could understand if I was terrible back to him, but I was so innocent towards him because I was taught to love "properly" at a young age and how to treat a partner with "love".

When drugs are used and needed daily, addiction begins and once you use them as an escape it's a band-aid for a bullet wound. The drug becomes your healing blanket. It's destructive and it became my undoing. Being so abused and so betrayed made my usage skyrocket. The more I became aware of what he was doing, knowing the deception he was capable of, the more it opened the door to the reality of what I was dragged into and I challenged him.

The more I stuck up for myself and questioned him, the more work I became to him, I started being a bigger problem. The next time he cheated on me was the day after Christmas. Christmas eve he said if I was to leave him alone and go to my mom's house, there's no telling who he would have to spend his time with and he made it clear he wasn't willing to come with me either. So I stayed. Devastated. Up to this point, I only did crystal meth, but he did Down (heroin) which I was SO against because when he did it ,he was a monster. I didn't allow it in my condo, he would use it with other people behind my back and disappear all the time. Finally, to get me to spend the money I had saved in my safe, on his drug of choice, he overdosed me on it by mixing it with the crystal meth that he was giving to me.

I woke up in the emergency room after being dead. After the first time I used it, I learned what it was to be Down sick and quickly became addicted. It was the ultimate numbing medication. Overdosing became a pattern for me at the beginning, the ambulance frequented my condo, he was careless with the amounts he gave me and I had no idea what I was doing.

We came to blows at this point, after everything he had done to me it started to eat me alive, my awareness heightened and it made me angry enough to fight back. He threatened to go after my parents, to fraud my parents if I didn't do what he wanted and he knew my family was of paramount importance to me. My relationship to my mother and father was special to me, that was my kryptonite. I did so much to protect them, to this day they still have no idea what I had to do. I was in constant anxiety and stress because our relationship was a rollercoaster from hell. It was so toxic. When others became aware of our fighting, they started to feel bad for me, people started to come to me in private and warn me about who Kyle really was. What he was known for in Vancouver.

Kyle pitched the idea of adding other men into our sexual relationship which killed me due to my history with Luke. Kyle decided to add one of my close trusted friends so it wouldn't be as hurtful. This friend accepted the offer but when we tried it, Kyle ironically overdosed on GHB so the threesome came to an early end. Mistakenly I thought that now Kyle had got the idea of adding someone to our bed out of his system, but a few days later, I learnt that he had cheated on me with this close friend on a night when I wasn't present. It was my friend that eventually confessed what they did together behind my back. He told me that Kyle was a manwhore, a "bottom slut".

These were terms I wasn't familiar with. The betrayal ate my friend alive, he hated that he betrayed my trust and even more because he hated the fact that he had even touched Kyle. My friend was high on GHB the night it happened, not that he used that as an excuse, but it did play a major part in altering his state of mind. If he hadn't been on the drug I don't think this friend would have done it to me. I was more upset because Kyle should have been the one to tell me, he is the one who was supposed to be with me.

It was this friend that helped me catch Kyle stealing my ID's and also showed me that Kyle had got a Cashmoney loan in my name with them. He set Kyle up and pretended to want to purchase the ID's off of him, Kyle wasn't aware that I knew about any of it. Kyle was super shocked to see me walk around the corner, with this friend, to meet up with him to buy the ID's off him. Kyle tried to twist and turn the story but I had already seen the text messages between them. My friend threatened to break Kyle's knee caps for being so evil towards me. This friend was the only one who told me what Kyle really was. Kyle held me close and tried to tell me that my friend was just trying to steal me away from him. It was clear to me that he was guilty and lying to me. He pulled this shit all the time. I would catch Kyle in lies all the time but I just wanted to believe the best in him, I was so pathetic. Love is powerful, love is blind.

Kyle picked stupid fights with me over nothing so he could disappear and do whatever he wanted. The drugs dulled my clarity and made me stupid. I was still uneducated in the dark side and I was all alone trying to fit in with people that simply weren't like me. I had never been or felt so alone. Isolated. Kyle assumed that everything I had was at his disposal, especially my car. One of the times he stole it, he ended up passing out, high at the wheel, and he hit an oncoming woman in a van. The police quickly arrived at the scene, found him running away and arrested him. Because it was my car and my insurance, I assumed the tickets and my car was towed to the nearest tow yard in Vancouver.

I received a phone call and was told my car was there, when I went to pick it up, the staff there seemed confused and couldn't locate my car. After getting management involved, I was told that the new owner of the car had come and picked it up. When they gave the person's name I called them and asked where my car was. I was told that I apparently took out a $15,000 equity loan at this person's loan company in Surrey. I signed a contract that stated in the event that I should default on the repayment schedule, I would sign over the ownership of my car as repayment. My stomach dropped and I almost fell over, I instantly knew what deception had taken place. Kyle had obtained this loan by impersonating me. I had no idea that he did this, there was no way I would ever do anything to lose my beloved car. I wouldn't trade it for anything, I was wrecked by this. This whole thing haunted me for weeks. The aftermath was colossal, I was so mad at Kyle.

Getting my license and having a car was a major pillar in my independence, I felt I was even more stuck. It was like my wings just got cut off. Of course I was also shocked and embarrassed if my family found out that my car was gone. I was afraid to call the police, Kyle had me believing that if I did, I would get arrested as well, because I was beside him while he committed the crimes. I was complicit. So he could do anything to me and never get in trouble.

Before I went to get my car that day, I bailed Kyle out of jail. I agreed to be his assurity and paid the court a thousand, so he could be released. So to find out that he betrayed me by giving my car away and I had just helped him with the courts, made me furious. Now we were joined by law and I was stuck with him and technically responsible for him, that's what being someone's assurity is. I didn't even want to be around him. The meaner I was to him, the more he would trump me, making my life worse.

My feelings weren't validated, I didn't have the energy to continue to be angry or even feel anything as a partner should. I was so alone and crushed. If he hadn't got me to be in love with him in the first place, I would have left so fast, before anything would have happened. He held my heart captive, the secret ingredient of total control was to gaslight me. He had spent all my money, compromised all my bank accounts, sold my expensive wardrobe, pawned my car and got me evicted from my place on Barclay Street. Luckily I was able to obtain a new place on Nicola Street. I hid this from him, I was so mad about what he had done to my car… to me. I tried to escape him.

No one really knew how bad it was, because in front of people he was nice to me, but behind closed doors I cried all the time. He would tell me to stop. I ran all around Vancouver confused, lost and afraid, hurt and alone, rigged with guilt and shame tormented with embarrassment. When other people started to see what he was doing to me they were like hyenas heckling me from afar. He knew my good and bad buttons to push so he always kept me on the hook, knowing which manipulative methods and weapons to use and how to use it.

The drugs mixed with this numbed out every situation and emotion. At this point it wasn't just my body physically needing Down, it was the lock and key to my chest of depression and anxiety. I was mortified to open it and terrified what I had become. I learned how to decompartmentalize my every emotion so no one understood me. The finality, to his wrath, was getting the VPD's glare to switch over from him to me, very craftily.

Eventually, after he stocked me, he found out where my place was on Nicola Street. He made my life beyond difficult, doing all sorts of terrible things to me and made it virtually impossible to save any of the money we were making to pay rent. He got me evicted from my place on Nicola Street. I became homeless and he left me all alone. He told me, "I can't be on the street Jeremy", which cut me deep for so many reasons. He started shacking up with one of his old clients that lived in a penthouse, somewhere I wasn't allowed to go. He had this guy all tangled up in his web of lies too. He committed fraud against him by stealing from his company, all the time. It was only when he would anger him and get himself kicked out that he would try and find me. I found out that he later killed this rich client in order to get his fortune. His wrath knew no bounds. The person I thought I loved was a wolf dressed in sheep skin. I was desperate to get my life back.

Kyle had told me that if I was to get a new vehicle he could be with me. So he gave me a guy's driver's license and told me to use it to purchase a BMW because that was his favorite.

He planned the whole thing and told me what I had to do which at the time elated me. I would have done anything to be with him, at this time, and not be alone on the streets. After all he did, I still told myself that I knew him, he loves me, maybe he was forced to do all of these horrible things to me? I wanted to believe my own made up conspiracy theories that I had made for him and I truly believed it for the longest time.

Kyle had me go into the BMW dealership and purchase a $45,000 car. He coached me, told me what to do and what to say and had me memorize all the details on the driver's license that he gave me so that I could successfully impersonate him. I went and bought the car one day and was told to come in the next day to insure it so I could drive it off the lot. Kyle told me I had to go in alone and to take a bag of fraud goods with me. He told me after I got the car I had to pick him up because we were doing another score. I went in, insured the car and was then given the keys by the salesman. I walked out the glass door of the dealership and went to the driver's side of the car. I clicked the unlock button on the keyfob and nothing happened. I realized the keyfob was for a Volkswagen, not a BMW. I looked up at the salesman who was still standing by the glass door, I will never forget the look on his face. It went from smiling goodbye to me, to a strict and stern glare. Suddenly there was a blast of dogs barking and helicopter noises, they paralyzed me. I swung my head around to the entrance of the dealership and a sea of police cars and uniformed men were running my way. The sirens rang through my body, it was piercing. I was dumbfounded. I can't explain the feeling, the shock and confusion, mixed with embarrassment - I knew I was caught. I had no idea what was going to happen to me, this was the first time I ever experienced the "kiss" of law enforcement. Kyle never told me what would happen if I was caught, he made it seem like that would never happen. When they searched my bag on the scene, they pulled out all the fraud items which made me look like some kingpin of fraud. I went from a "regular" citizen to a terrible criminal faster than I could blink. When they cuffed me and threw me in the police wagon, I was bawling my eyes out, confused, lost and afraid. Everything started making sense, why Kyle didn't want to actually come with me to the dealership and why he gave me the bag instead of keeping it himself. At the time when he was preparing me to go get the car, it did seem odd but I just didn't think he would ever set me up. I didn't even know people could collaborate with the police to do something like this. This made me question everything I ever thought I knew about love. I was stunned, but I wasn't surprised. Forget about love, for Kyle to do this to me meant he clearly didn't even like me. My foolish heart.

It felt like I was in a horror movie. Playing with someone's mind is one thing, but playing with someone's heart in my opinion is a whole other atrocity of evil. I felt like I was kicked in the balls and nailed in the stomach. The corruption rang through my body. It made my blood boil.

My heart was completely destroyed, broken into a million pieces and stomped on. It was when I got to jail and started sharing with the other inmates as to why I was there and what had happened at the BMW dealership that I discovered what Kyle had done to me. Everyone reacted with shock and their jaws dropped. They all said the same thing, I was clearly a mark to Kyle. I then explained all the underhanded things he had done to me, each one told me what they meant.

People had heard about Kyle in jail, and his reputation was not good. Mine took a hit when I started dating him. He did warn me actually. Which was true, all my clients that always had great trusting relationships with me suddenly looked at me differently. They treated me oddly. I felt like I was just a skeleton that lost its skin. Everything I've ever believed in, what I thought of humanity, was uprooted and destroyed. I really can't put enough words together to illustrate how betrayed I felt. How humiliated I felt. What an idiot I was. Plus I had only methadone to help my suffering while in jail so I was basically forced into sobriety and forced to face all the many emotions I had been suppressing. This jail stint was my first, and it lasted six months.

The only thing and the only way you can try to understand me is to imagine your current partner doing this to you. How hurt would you be? Now my wounds were oozing and in pain, I was desperate for my crutch, drugs. Once I had been introduced to this powerful band-aid to mend my feelings it was my go-to for pain. Letting in and dealing with everything that had occurred to me in the past years broke me down. Everything he had ever said to me was literally a lie. He called my parents told them I was on drugs, shooting up, and hooking on the streets and then tried telling them I was defrauding them.

Whenever I didn't do what he wanted, that was his threat, because he knew that was my main vein. Over my dead body would I ever allow it. I had to learn his craft in order to stop it. It was so serious that when I called anti-fraud Canada they suggested changing my name and sin number. He had stolen my everything but worst of all, finding out how corrupt this world is, the reality that some humans are capable of such evil really jaded my mind even more. I was using Down at this point to get through the day.

One of the most serious situations that I had to deal with, which added a lot of darkness to my already jaded mind, was a rumor that swirled around downtown Vancouver about a crackhead woman, a mother, who had two kids, one girl, 10 and a boy 8. She sold her kids to an older man, a pedophile.

There was one billionaire client ,that I saw quite a few times, who would hire me and come over to my place. I had for security purposes the Telus alarm system installed in my apartment. It came with full surveillance. I would often get calls and texts from people wanting to book with me, but this one time the person was requesting to just come to talk to me and they were quite aggressive. He said it was urgent. This person somehow knew that the billionaire client of mine was regularly booking with me. When he questioned me about this client I said I couldn't disclose anything, information and I told him I couldn't help.

There are always questions and inquiries that I was asked while booking. This guy kept asking if I only did 1 on 1 or if I allowed certain kinks to take place, I said it depended on what they were.

When they finally booked with me, he showed up and didn't appear like he was actually looking for services. He was rugged. He happened to come by right after this billionaire client left my place after a session with him. I could tell that this guy meant business. He asked me if I heard about that mother that sold her two underage children to some billionaire tycoon. My stomach dropped, I have lots of clients but not many billionaires, so I knew who he was talking about.

He asked me if the billionaire ever brought kids to our sessions. I was outraged and mortified. The weight of confusion hung in the air. The thought of this was vile and disgusting and there is know way I would ever allow such a thing to happen. This individual wanted me to prove to him that this client always came alone. So I showed him the video footage that automatically saves from my Telus system, so he could see that this billionaire client only ever entered the front door alone. His questioning was hostile, but I understood given the allegations.

I really don't understand how any human can be attracted sexually to children, it is baffling to me, a horrifying thought. In the escort world, the rule is never to steal from clients or hurt them. Never do them dirty, as word will spread and you won't get booked anymore. I was cautious and tried to be delicate about every situation. The man left and I thought that it was over, until the next day, he contacted me again insisting that he required my further assistance.

Because everyone downtown was out looking for this crackhead mother, and it seemed she couldn't be found, a group of individuals decided to go through me. I was approached by the group of people to orchestrate an event to "hurt" one of my clients: this billionaire pedophile. The group contact came back over, but this time he wasn't alone. There was a group of men who came with him. I experienced some major ptsd when I opened that door to find a bunch of men standing there. They forced themselves in and sat me down. I was shown some evidence towards the allegations, they had the mother's bank statements that showed a large sum of money deposited into her account and there were photos of the children entering this billionaire's mansion. It became clear they wanted to get this "guy" and save the kids. Usually I wouldn't have wanted any involvement, but it didn't really appear that I had a choice. This "gang" was well known for their lack of respect for life. My chest tightened and my mind raced. I felt very claustrophobic. They asked me to book this client for an "out" call, in doing this it would give them a window of opportunity to get into his gated mansion.

I knew the gate code to his place because when he would book me I would have to enter to get inside. I let them know if they were going to do anything drastic they should do their due diligence to make sure that the children were actually there. I asked them to make sure, because of the possibilities that it was just a rumor or maybe the mother and this billionaire knew each other from the past so he would watch the children. I dropped a hint about involving social services but I got a look from the group and they made it perfectly clear that if I was to talk, I would be next.

To justify their suspicions one of the group showed me a confession video of this mother admitting what she had done to get a huge payout, showing the power of drugs and how destructive they can be. This evidence fucked me up for a long time. I felt dirty knowing that I let this man touch me, since he was actively involved with trafficking children. Why did I end up getting involved? This made me throw up. I ended up hitting the pipe really hard to try to forget. I also felt ill because I was going to be part of another man's death.

I felt forced to collaborate with this gang. Many would argue that any person who sexually abuses children deserves to die, but I am not saying that, I don't agree but I am very against anything involving a child and sex. Those two words shouldn't never be put together, in my opinion. However, I wish the situation was different, I wish I wasn't forced to play a part in their scheme that cost the billionaire his life. On a human level, when I face my creator at the end of my life, I wish I wouldn't have the deception of the client, even if he is a guilty human being. I just wish I didn't have any of this on my rap sheet, but I am glad that he will never get the chance to hurt other innocent children. I don't truly know what happened to the mother of these poor children or my billionaire client…they just disappeared after all this. I never mentioned this to anyone, until now.

My addiction was now at its highest level and I was surrounded by individuals that thought that this way of life with crime was acceptable which only confused my thought process. Drugs made everything acceptable. It was the perfect denial and remedy. Everything that happened to me took place while on drugs, it was the fuel.

Every addict needs to make money, every day, to supplement their addiction, the majority don't have jobs and they are desperate. This makes everyone a target in downtown Vancouver and anything that's not glued to your body is up for the taking. Crime is a side effect of addiction. I've had so many bags, phones, clothes, drugs and money stolen from me throughout the years. It's extremely hard to not have the attitude of "fuck it, if I can't beat em", so that's what I did I joined em! I thought, well they did it to me or it happened to me so I have the right to do it to other people, the universe owes me.

The people in this dark world baited me. They would set me up or push me to my breaking point then I'd do something to fight back just so they could gain some reason just to get gunned down ten times worse. People would hire people to do all kinds of terrible things. Hurt people, hurt people. There isn't a book full of instructions and pro tips on what to do and what to not to do while trying to survive in this environment. I've witnessed people being murdered, committing suicide, I have been in the same vehicle as a hitman and I've walked with men in all of the different gangs. I've seen the rich commit crimes, almost killing me and handing an envelope full of money to silence the police on the scene and everyone prayed on my lack of knowledge to get away with the atrocities. That's why they say "knowledge is power" but being so "powerful" now, ironically, I've never felt more powerless.

No one has respect for life, overdosing on drugs in Vancouver isn't even investigated. There are so many things I was exposed to that left me in disbelief that it was actually happening. This makes a hitman's job of killing someone very easy. It also makes trying to survive among it all, extremely dangerous. Anyone that came into my life was not random. People heard that I was this "talented idiot" that others could fake "a friendship" with then wait for me to score and make money. After I did this they would strike, kick the shit out of me and take whatever I had. At one point I was given housing in an SRO but when people knew where to find me, I became an easy target. It got to a point that being homeless on the street was a better option ,this says a lot.

I developed into one of the top fraudsters in Vancouver, as being so addicted to Down, made it impossible to escort. I had to take a criminal approach to making money to support my drug habit. I still had certain restrictions and boundaries certain things I wouldn't do. Everyone's loyalty depends on their mental state and how desperate they are that day to get drugs. It felt like friendship and loyalty had a price and anyone could be bought no matter how deep the bond made with them was.

I couldn't depend on anyone or anything, everything was synthetic and everyone knew everybody. It's like they hate and hurt each other by day, but they all come together and sit at the dinner table at night as family members. It was so confusing. I never knew who was secretly involved with who.

After doing my first six month jail time for the BMW fiasco, was when I realized that I didn't want to join them or be like them. As much as I wanted to strike back it only made things worse for me. I didn't want to be hated any more than everyone already did, that's the norm in downtown Vancouver.

Everyone has a reason to be evil or bad, everyone has a reason to be a bitch, so I learnt to not take it personally. My compassion and empathy made me weak in this atmosphere in this environment. Every time I would get out of jail over the four years, I would get updated when I returned to downtown Vancouver. Everything that took place during my incarceration: Who robbed who, who got put in jail and who set who up.

Ironically this was the best news for me, it changed my way of thinking. I always took everything so personal, but now I knew it wasn't. If it wasn't me as the target, it would have been somebody else. I decided I wasn't going to be anything like them, as they were rotten. No one wants to have the reputation of being a "piece of shit" in this dark part of the world, but that doesn't mean I have to be too.

Make no mistake, I do not judge because I was one of them. I did lots of different fraud crimes. One of the times I was arrested because I was impersonating a guy, I had his ID's and memorized everything about him and accessed his credit bureau. I went into Scotiabank and opened up a new checking account with a $10,000 overdraft and opened a $20,000 line of credit. My rule was anything I did needed to be insured, the person whose ID's I was using needed to be able to declare fraud and have it wiped off their bureau. The banker set up a new card for me and I set the new pin. I didn't know that they had automatically sent a message to his old email on file, from previous banking history, congratulating him on his new accounts, clearly he acted quickly. I was on my way out of the bank when suddenly the actual guy whose ID's I had was on the other side of the glass bank doors holding them closed.

Ironically, or thankfully, I looked more like him than he did, so I told the bankers that he was an imposter and an ex boyfriend who was stalking me. When he came into the bank and confronted me, the bank staff believed me and let me leave. As I quickly walked away from the bank, I turned around and realized he was chasing me while on the phone with the police.

I ran up zig zagging through 20 blocks from 2nd avenue in Vancouver all the way up to the SkyTrain. I was going through different back doors of buildings trying to escape. I could hear the sirens, I was so exhausted that I finally collapsed in the back of a moving truck. The police surrounded the truck and yelled at me to come out but I couldn't move, I was exhausted. They threatened to send the dogs in. I yelled at them and told them I couldn't move as I layed on my stomach.

They jumped into the back of the truck and started kicking and hitting me. They screamed, telling me to put my arms behind my back but two of them were standing on my arms ,purposefully, so I couldn't. One of them had me in a stranglehold, so I couldn't speak or yell for help. A pedestrian stood watching, pulled out her phone and threatened them to stop or she was going to report the video she was recording. They let up, finally, allowing me to put my hands behind my back and I gasped for air.

Looking back, I don't know why I didn't attack the boy following me, maybe I felt guilty or that I knew I wasn't a slime. He certainly didn't deserve getting his "ass kicked", I did.

I got the shit kicked out of me by the Vancouver police all the time. The police have done many things to me that I don't believe are legal or ethical but they don't have much sympathy for drug addicts or criminals. It's not like I was violent, I weighed 100 lbs. I was no match for them. The VPD attacked me all the time, any chance they would get me behind closed doors, especially in city cells. City cells are where they take anyone who is arrested at first for processing. When I was arrested they would bring me there overnight, abusing me and treating me like scum of the earth. The next day I would obtain a legal aid lawyer to go in front of a judge and apply for bail. The whole experience is hell, especially because I would go into withdrawal each time. I would get bail every time, until the 8th or 9th time of being there, that's when the courts started remanding me, a whole different sort of hell. When I was remanded, I was forced to go to North Fraser Pretrial Centre and each time the stay started getting longer and longer, more serious each time. Its the courts way of saying you've fucked up too many times so we are going to start punishing you. Before these experiences, I never would have thought that I would get abused by the police. Individuals who hold a high position in society and who are supposed to protect all citizens, not just the ones they choose to. Nothing is ever as it seems, from the bottom of society to the top. Society thinks it's the homeless criminals who are the bad law breakers and doing all the crimes; that they are the problem. However, often the people in suits are the real criminals taking part in the big scandals. They are so well protected in whatever high position they hold in society, they are untouchable. It is so corrupt, everything is so backwards.

Addiction became my comfort zone. It made all my dark thoughts go and eased my grieving. Kyle would kick my grieving in the ass and laugh at it. When I would sit alone and start to reflect and think about something he had done to me, I'd cry. So I packed my pipe and smoked it and - boom - it was gone. He made my life hell and unfortunately my life was stuck on autopilot. I was so immune to the suffering. I was living in constant fear and anxiety, a hell few have ever heard of. A place of confusion, depression, devastation, darkness, loneliness and so many more bitterly sharp adjectives. The dark side of the world, the underbelly of city life and the devastation of some of humanity's deepest atrocities, the devil's malicious teachings that make us capable of extraordinary tragic and pitiful actions. The downfall of addiction, the hidden employments, the masterminds of deception, the underground rules and money making schemes as addicts use and abuse the humans close to them for their sick desires. The power of manipulation, the wrongly used tool of love that quite literally people use as a weapon as they undo your life and take away from you, everything you are.

Addicts are never at peace and don't stop, they are forever restless. I felt like I was always playing catch up. Drugs made everything bearable, that is how I felt. I was so internally damaged that drugs became my lifeline, it made me more of an addict, shame and guilt crippled me because I knew my family and society looked down on me for using drugs. I didn't care, I didn't need anyone as long as I had my drugs. The heavier I felt the more I used so it became a double-edged sword without escape. I lost hope. I didn't believe in faith because, if there were a god, how could he let all the shady shit happen to me and other people? It made me doubt his existence.

Mental illness is called an illness for a reason. When someone gets cancer, you can't say well it's a choice - just decide to not be ill anymore and that's all it takes. This is the exact same thing as telling an addict just don't do drugs and choose to be healed. It's not that easy. Addiction, the drugs, were now very interconnected with my emotions and feelings and had become my faith, my truth.

My thought process at that time was at least I could see the drugs working so I knew it was real, unlike my faith in god. Every deception cut so deep. I could do drugs and function enough to feel I could keep it up. I was working so hard to prove to my family and everyone who wronged me, and myself, that I finally knew now what this sinister game was and I was going to get my life back. I finally knew what the fuck was going on after spending so much time running around looking for answers from a bunch of hyenas. Doing drugs and having a goal is like trying to walk up an icy hill. It's just not possible. I can't unsee what I know now, the exposure is so aggressive. I felt so demoralized.

There were times in jail where I was treated like an animal. The guards are terrible, the other inmates range from being decent to horrible. What little rights I did have were taken away and my privacy even more invaded. I had to use the bathroom in a cell with a metal toilet in front of another person and vice versa. It was so dehumanizing to me. No one seemed bothered that I was incarcerated.

My mother was happy because she knew I was safely alive at least and sober while I was incarcerated. Her attitude felt like a stab in the back at the time. It wasn't until I was arrested for my last stunt ,which put me in here this time ,that I started to understand her way of thinking.

Everything was a first to me, each tragedy and calamity. Every day I became more and more estranged to myself and became someone I didn't know, my shine was so dulled out. There was no laughter, the odd time I did laugh my face would hurt because my cheeks were so rarely uplifted. I knew being on drugs was no way of life but I liked that any failures that came my way got a pass, a mulligan due to drugs, as it eradicated all my depressed thoughts. The mind is such a powerful thing and I've spent years now telling myself I needed them to survive which made any chance of recovery complicated, making my addiction even more difficult to stop. Stopping meant having to deal with all my oppressed broken emotions and relive everything I have spent years trying to convince myself didn't actually happen. I had every shocking situation that surfaced in my life tucked and tidied so neatly compartmentalized hidden away in the deepest places of my mind. Quitting them meant rewiring my mind and I didn't think I was the right technician for the job.

I truly thought that I wasn't going to get out alive, out of this mess. My continued depression led my thoughts to dark places. I wondered if my family wished I would just die, so they didn't have to watch or be in pain while dealing with me. I felt like I was missing out on so much, my younger siblings were getting older and my mom entering her golden years, something that caused pain everyday. I was just so angry with the reality that I was completely used by Kyle. Used is an understatement. When I finally knew who he really was, we were over, he figured I had nothing to offer him, nothing of value for him to use, his focus shifted elsewhere. I still would see him around town and he would try to bewitch me again. The mind games he played, acting like he cared here and there, toying with my mind, it took a long time until I finally understood how he truly viewed me.

Once I started to be a slave to Down, I started to become like him, the drug changed me for the worse. I started to act like him, coming and going in and out of people's lives using them to a certain degree. I just started to understand that Down took priority over everything I did in a day and how I treated people. But I refused to do any of the really horrible things that he had done to me, to other people. Sometimes to get to the light, we have to touch darkness. What I was willing to do to get drugs, commit crime, break the law and literally spend every dollar on it, including my rental portion from my disability cheque, which made me homeless on Hastings Street. It was my king and I was his servant.

One of the many problems with being a lover and not a fighter in this dark side of the world was I got pushed around a lot and my desperation put me in so many compromising situations and lowered my standard of acceptable living situations to an all time low. One of the worst situations that I got myself into was being kidnapped. I was walking down a dark road late at night downtown in English Bay. A van screeched to a stop beside me. Before I could react, two men in dark clothes and ski masks grabbed me, shoved me into the back of the van. The door slammed shut and I was plunged into darkness. The van lurched forward, I felt a sharp, cold object pressed against the side of my head. Feeling it made my heart stop. The ride seemed to last forever, the van bumped over rough roads until it finally came to a halt. The men yanked me out and dragged me into a basement of a house, the air inside was thick with the smell of dust and drugs. They threw me into a chair and tied me down, secured my wrists and ankles with rough rope. I struggled, but the bonds held tight. A third man entered, his face partially hidden in the shadow of his baseball cap. He looked calm, almost bored, as he approached me. "You're a fraudster, right?" the man asked, his voice too calm, too casual for the situation. I nodded, my throat was too dry to speak. "Good. We need your skills". The man tossed a laptop onto the table in front of me, then produced a handgun from his waistband, placing it on the table as well, just within my reach, but close enough to be an ever-present threat. The man's gaze was cold as he continued. "You're going to create some money for us.

Quietly. Quickly. And without a trace. You do this, and maybe you'll leave us
alive."

 My hands shook as they untied me, the bruises forming on my wrists as I fumbled to open the laptop. I was surrounded by men, each one with a gun, their eyes never left me. Escape was impossible; I had no choice but to comply. They told me what to do, who the accounts belonged to, and how to manipulate the systems so the money would vanish, leaving no trail. I was good at my job- too good, it seemed. The work was horrifyingly easy, my fingers moved across the keyboard almost automatically, as if my mind had detached from the nightmare I was living. As I worked, time lost all meaning. Hours blurred into each other, the only constant being the gun on the table and the cold eyes watching my every move. They fed me just enough Down to keep me from being sick. The sums of money were staggering, amounts I could barely comprehend, transferred with a few keystrokes from one company to another, and then the accounts that would be wiped clean before anyone noticed. I was to set up a $200,000 TD line of credit under a profile that looked like me, that was the last thing I was to complete. But it wasn't just fraud. The man in the baseball cap wanted more. He made me hack into systems, change records, erase debt- destroy lives with a few clicks. Each action dug deeper into my soul, leaving behind a growing void of guilt and despair. Every now and then, the man would lean closer, his voice in a low whisper in my ear. "Remember, you fuck up, you die. You try to alert anyone, you die. Your family? We know where they live. They'll die too." My hands were slick with sweat, my vision blurring with exhaustion, but I kept going. I had no choice. My thoughts circled endlessly, trying to find a way out, a way to survive the nightmare without destroying myself in the process. But the walls closed in with every passing moment. Finally, after what felt like days, I could see the sun was now up, the man in the cap nodded. "That's enough", he grabbed the laptop and looked at all the work I did and made sure the TD line of credit was done properly. "You did good, real good. Now you are going to get yourself together and we will walk you to the TD bank down the road and you will use this ID that looks like you and make a withdrawal from the line of credit you just created." They marched me down everyday with a gun to my back, making me risk jail time and my freedom. I would enter the bank alone, go up to the bank teller, pull the money out, exit the bank and give the guys the money and then they would walk me back and put me in their basement until the sun rose the next day. I was shaking with anxiety and riddled with fear. They barely fed me anything other than drugs to keep me going.

Whenever I protested or said I wouldn't do it, they just pulled the gun out and pointed it at my head. After the 3rd day in a row, the bank teller finally was worried because I couldn't hide the fact that I looked like I feared for my life. They could tell something was up, I looked disheveled. They finally asked me if I was in trouble or if I was being forced into doing this? I had a panic attack, dropped to the ground and had a seizure. I woke up in the emergency room but thankfully it allowed me to escape this group of guys. I felt like a pawn in a game I could never win and somewhere out there, the man would be waiting, watching, ready to pull me back into the darkness the moment I slipped up or was sighted by the wrong people. This time it was a different kind of feeling, of being used.

It became apparent that because I did crystal meth and Down it made me a target for bad people to use my addiction as a weapon against me. I had to be extremely careful with who I worked with or who I told anything to. Living on Hastings Street, being homeless, felt like admitting defeat. The morning air on Hastings Street was thick with a chill that seeped through my bones. Even in the summer, there's a dampness that clings to everything- the pavement, the buildings, my clothes. I would wake up on the concrete, my back aching from another night spent trying to find comfort on something so unforgiving. The noise of the city was my alarm clock: the rumble of trucks, the distant chatter of early morning commuters, the occasional siren that reminded me help is never coming for me. My world was a small space- just a few feet of sidewalk that I claimed as my own, marked by the few possessions I still had. I would always think that I used to be someone, someone with a name, a job, a home. But now, here on Hastings, I am just another face in a sea of forgotten souls. The worst part was the fear- fear of what I have become, fear of what I might do to survive another day, fear that I'll never escape this place, this life. Hastings is a trap, and once you're caught, it's almost impossible to get out. But I kept moving because stopping means giving up, and I will never give up hope. I clung onto it like a religion, knowing it's the only thing standing between me and the abyss. I would always tell people, when I was asked, that I was in between places but never admitted to being homeless, especially to my family.

It's a dog eat dog world living homeless downtown. The city tries to make it possible with free food trucks from time to time, safe injection sites and lots of government poverty Help Centers. The streets transform at night, the shadows lengthen and temperature drops. The fact that, in the back of my mind, I knew I had nothing, living on the street with a multitude of terribly violent, scary people, I would use even more drugs to function day to day and to accept the fact that this now was my life.

I was in so deep, I didn't even know where to start or how to get back what I had lost. I met an older 64 year old man who I became quite close with, he took me in off the street. He lived in a nice tall apartment building, right in the middle of Gayville. I loved it. I was so grateful for him, I had a deep respect and admiration for him because he saved me. I was so beaten and battered from living on the streets and the wounds from Kyle were still gaping. At first it wasn't romantic, but we grew so close. He did a lot for me and I for him, when I had the capacity to. I didn't think he knew about the dark side of the world. I knew he was sexual and did crystal meth, but he was proper, he didn't conduct himself like a drug addict. He fell in love with me, but my heart was still very much destroyed and I wasn't particularly attracted to older men. Nonetheless, I did have a strong feeling for him, maybe because of my circumstances or the fact that he also had a bubbly personality, full of love and laughter, when he wanted to be. I did end up in jail a few times, while I was living with this older man. Every time I was released I would do drugs immediately while living with him. We did click, personality-wise and we just seemed to fit into each other's lives at that moment in time. The sweet turned to sour, we began to fight like cats and dogs. I still had a deep respect for him because he gave me a semi-safe place to live and stay. He fed me and helped me pay for my Down addiction. He always had crystal meth on him, which at that time made him very attractive to me. Anytime I left his house though all hell broke loose. At the beginning he would come with me to get Down and I loved that he did, but then the novelty wore off.

He wanted to control me. He would send me paragraphs of text messages and phone calls when I wasn't home. He would call me names, swear and threaten. I only left the house to get drugs, which I had to do daily, this bothered him. He was a jealous man. What he would say to me was completely unacceptable. I honestly never wasn't there because I was hooking up with someone else, even though technically I wasn't obligated to him. His anger was very misplaced.

I felt wronged and controlled. I was taught that this kind of behavior was not okay, I was taught to treat the people I like and love with respect at all times. I didn't call my friends names or swear at them. I was conflicted and stuck. As soon as I returned, he would act as if nothing happened and he was never accountable for his behavior. I knew that doing nothing wasn't a proper way to conduct myself, but I couldn't stick up for myself, I really depended on him, so I had to play to the beat of his drum.

The "normal" me, before all this chaos, wouldn't have any relationship with a man of his age or his way of life. It showed how mentally and emotionally fucked up I was.

So there I was again, doing something and being somewhere I knew I wouldn't be caught dead doing, if I was in my "normal" state of mind. I say having my feelings and emotions validated by others is extremely important but validating them myself is key. The more I didn't do what I thought I knew I should, the more I let myself down, the more emotionally distraught I got.

Letting someone see me naked and sharing intimate moments unnaturally was extremely poisonous to my soul. I was suffocating and everyone around me talked down to me, as if they all were trying to convince me that I deserved it and they knew me, when I know that no one that crossed paths with me during this time actually knew the real me as the real me would never have been there. I thought this older man was innocent, not a part of the dark side of the world but little by little I became aware.

He had given me the wrong name from the beginning. He lied about his life prior to meeting me and he experimented in crime and gaslighting people. He knew the craft of deception and was well known by the other fraudsters I knew. So yet again, right when I was putting my guard down, I was clobbered. I had been living with a man that lied about everything to try to get me to fall for him. Drugs, my pipe, were the only things I could count on.

This older man enabled me, in hindsight. During this period, what Kyle did to me became legendary. I was the poor son of a bitch that got fucked over by his own heart. I was lonely, dying to meet someone my own age. A year after living with this older man, I did a score with Kyle, after running into him on the street when I went down to the ministries office to get my monthly cheque. Through this score I met a drug dealer named Rob, but his nickname was Batman. We hit it off, he was only a couple years older than me. We had a "thing" for six months, it gave me life and hope once again. This feeling was short lived: I found out that not only was he a drug dealer, but he was a hitman, and had a girlfriend who was very well known within gangs the entire time that we were together. That being involved in a gay relationship would ruin his reputation. One of my close friends that knew of him took me aside and told me something about Batman that changed everything.

Apparently he had kidnapped two kids in Kamloops; they turned out to be the kids of a gang member in the Hells Angels. He moved to downtown Vancouver and implanted himself in Gayville to hide. I had no idea who he really was, yet again I was deceived and my heart was wrong. I couldn't catch a break. The drama that he put me through was explosive.

At this point disappointment started to become a regular feeling. I got picked up on a warrant, shortly after me and Rob officially ended our relationship. When I was put in jail, I joined bible study and practiced the lessons. Part of AA and NA relate to the bible, so I wanted to understand it. I feel like anything that helped someone to be successful with beating this disease is something worth looking into. I had already overdosed seven times, each time I was "electrified" back to life in the emergency room. I now believe God is working through me and has exposed me to all these awful things because I am meant to do more for this world.

People think of addiction as only being associated with drugs, alcohol and smoking. Wrong. People I've met have had trouble with being addicted to: people, places, things, candy (food), gambling, shopping, collecting and hoarding material things, and so much more.

The other element that shocked me was the kinds of people that sat in AA or NA rooms. The people were of every dynamic: sexuality, race, sex, shape, size, success and nationality. Addicts can be successful business people with good jobs of all sorts, which is why I never judge a book by its cover anymore. I would do well in jail and tell my family that I would stay sober but when I got released, each time I would just run back to the older man's house to get higher than a kite.

I've always had this special, magnificent imagery, a vision of myself and my own addiction and what that looks like to me. In my mind I picture myself as this little boy sitting on a park bench surrounded by darkness, lost in the abyss. He is so scared, he sits there crying with his hands covering his face, he is too terrified to look up. The monsters that surround him are every trauma he's endured during his addiction. All the bad things, every broken heart. He's so fragile, it's so intimate. He's shattered and drowning in hopelessness. Unfortunately, everytime he tries to be brave, he is struck down by a new monster. It's really sad and emotional. He is paralyzed with fear and doubt. His bravery has been stolen away and courage taken. Recovery and sobriety, is holding out his hand telling him it's okay, we can do this, just grab my hand I'll pull you away and protect you. You can do it.

Me facing my trauma and addiction is the little boy and whether or not he will find the courage and strength to grab my hand and listen to sobriety. Recovery depends on whether or not I will stay sober and really find hope and faith again but most importantly if I can stop and face my trauma.

It's ironic that what will heal me is being able to validate myself, not get it from someone else. To educate myself. To repent on my sins and to seek forgiveness from the ones I hurt, to make amends to my family and anyone that was negatively affected.

I needed to learn how to get rid of my guilt and shame, they pour gas on the fire. They make me feel heavy and it makes me want to use drugs more. The final time I got arrested on Jan 16, 2024 forced me to be sober and away from all my triggers, negative people, the environment I was flailing in. It would have been substantially harder, if not harder, probably impossible to stay off drugs, had I not been arrested. To give myself credit, I have been offered drugs and they do offer methadone in jail, which is a synthetic legal opioid, by the government but I've personally chosen to wean off of it and have denied all drug offers. So I am proud because I felt like this time I was willing to find a positive, and in doing that, sobriety became my silver lining within the bars.

Recovery and treatment centers take an addict away from the environment they've been living in, it can make sobriety humanly possible, if you were out on the streets downtown Vancouver on your own, there's no way to stay sober. I personally wouldn't have had the chance to write a book, decide to make a change, participate in bible studies and AA/NA programs, if arrest didn't happen. Jail is saving me, but I had to be willing to utilize the time wisely, instead of hating my life and planning my return to the streets with drugs.

A few years previous, before my final time in-jail, I did accept an offer of Down. I sniffed way too much of it, unaware of the proper amount, they found me dead in my cell. Code blue was called, a medical emergency and I woke up in the "seg" unit. The other time I tried to smoke down using a laptop cord, tinfoil from peanut butter seal, two leads from a pencil to create a spark with a carefully twisted up paper towel as a wick and I electrocuted myself in the cell. I went flying across the room and all the TVs on the unit went out because I tripped the breaker. There were a lot of "pissed off" guys, at me, in the morning. I didn't get high that night. I didn't try it again. It was like the universe was telling me to STOP.

I started a great crusade in writing a book, everyone told me to journal my thoughts and feelings so that I could get it out of my system while I was in jail this time. I was told continually that my story was a story that needed to be heard. My thoughts, when we as humans experience trauma, or hardship, the idea is to "get it out". For some that may struggle with reading and writing, they may choose to go to counseling. Everyone's way of healing is different and very individualized, but the idea is the same. Whether you are a writer, like me or getting a professional counselor to validate you in a session, it all comes down to validation in my opinion.

Bible study taught me to repent, shed light on my troubles and hand it over to Jesus, our lord. For the record, I'm no "bible thumper". I'm quite skeptical and somewhat a realist, but I do believe in the magic and spirituality in the world. Even with the knowledge I now have, I still have my reservations, however the fundamentals, lessons and ideals in the bible are fantastic. Just as AA and NA, the 12 steps are of paramount importance. I don't really have a set religion nor was one ever forced on me, I just know that I like what I've learnt, the positive studies, and the offering of so many ways to help someone in need. When I read the big book of AA I felt like it was talking directly to me. I love that.

Every drug addict, me, is in desperate need of a new set of tools. I don't want to make the book I wrote about religion nor would I push it on anyone and if I'm being perfectly honest, religion was only a very small part of my miraculous recovery. I just wanted to share what I was doing and my findings in what was working for me.

This brings me back to my next love, Jason. Everything up to this current jail time, and after Kyle, I was living with the older man until I met Jason. Jason and I were given a room each in the SRO where I had previously lived, but left because it was too dangerous. However, they did a major house cleaning, new staff, new upgrades and a lot of the terrible people that were occupying it back then either left or were evicted. I thought that I would try it again, especially because I felt having Jason in the same building would make it safer. I was right, for the most part. I was very deep into my addiction. I was craving someone my own age after "Batman" had disappeared after being confronted regarding the kidnapping. He threatened my life if I ever spoke of it again, which confirmed it for me, I was out after that. I found out later Batman was murdered in jail some time after.

I met Jason online, he was from Ontario. Our relationship had its ups and downs. During our honeymoon phase, everything was great. There were some mood swings and something was a bit off about him, which, at first, I thought was sexy and mysterious. But as time went on our relationship started to have its ups and downs. When we first met he had a couple of different guys, here and there. We were casual so it didn't bother me. Now… looking back, I can see that he was using these guys for different reasons which was a common thing to do in this world, using connections and resources that people you would meet to your advantage. One had a car, one had his own place that he seemed to flip from, back and forth. When we started to hang out more often, I believed we were getting closer, but then one night he randomly attacked me, unprovoked. It scared the "shit" out of me, and through what I knew about neuro divergence, seemed very bi-polar. I had experienced some physical abuse with Kyle, but nothing like this where he just suddenly came at me. Thankfully I was able to escape the house we were at, he had been staying with a man from Aldergrove. I was in shock by the violence, but he messaged me right away, asking where I was and apologizing. He justified his behavior by saying he was trying to push me away because he was falling for me. I should have known then, but I stayed. We had our issues, it was dysfunctional, the need for drugs became the primary reason we would come together. When it was good with him, it was GREAT, but when it was bad with him, it was HORRIBLE. When his family came down for his birthday and we had been dating for quite some time, he proposed to me in Vancouver while his family was present to witness.

He continued to attack me a few times during our relationship. I was shocked each time because we were in love and that's not what I wanted love to be. He would tell me he was trying to push me away because he was scared to open up to me each time. Since when is it okay to attack the one you love? I witnessed this many times while I lived on the streets downtown Vancouver. So many couples fight and hate on each other, they call each other every name under the sun and come to blows. Straight, gay or lesbian, it doesn't matter, it was all the same especially when both parties were on drugs.

I assumed anyone from Vancouver city knew "the game" so they couldn't be trusted. I was too scared. I figured that Jason wasn't from here so maybe he would be different. I think he has the potential to be a great partner, but clearly had trauma of his own to deal with. That trauma carried into our relationship.

He cheated on me, lied to me and let me down countless times. He had mood swings that confused me. He was really good at being a lover when he wanted to be. I still don't know if he is a "Kyle". That's what I call someone who is evil and relates to all the awful things that Kyle did to me. We fought about this saying because when he did something or said something like what Kyle had done to me and made me cry, I would call him Kyle and he would get super offended. I did allude to Jason the details of what Kyle had done to me as I was very much damaged goods. He knew my triggers but he still was careless with me.

After Jason was violent with me, he would act like it didn't happen and would be exceptionally nice. This threw me off, but because I was exposed to this type of abusive relationship in the past, I let it slide. He was not a good partner, but I felt that his past relationships had made him this way along with this addiction-fast-forward, anxiety-filled world as well. We were two passing ships trying to cope with the thralls of being drug addicts.

He was all I knew and I am glad I was with him during the last couple of years of chaos. I don't regret anything because I saw the beauty in him. In our intimate moments, when it was just me and him, eye to eye, we got along and laughed all the time. But with him, I just felt like I never really knew what he was thinking.

It was hard maintaining a healthy relationship when we both were taking a drug that inspires selfishness. I did catch him talking about me to his friend from Ontario, I didn't care much for her. Jason and I lived together in an SRO on Burrard Street downtown Vancouver at first, together. It was an awful canary yellow inside. I went there after one of my jail stints. We thought that a friend of his was stealing from me. My wallet and watch went missing. It turned out that the friend was the one from Ontario. She also set us up and

got two guys to rob us after Jason hit her in the face after some altercation between the two of them. They had a very odd friendship. My computers and my bags were stolen, I was choked. But he still kept her around which didn't make sense.

I began to question him in my mind, which hurt, because I loved him and didn't want to believe it. One time I pretended to go to the bathroom and closed the door to our apartment behind me. The bathrooms were shared for each floor so I had to leave our place to go to it. The walls were paper thin and I wanted to see if they would talk about me. I stayed and listened from outside the door. I will never forget what I heard that night.

He began talking in a darker tone, telling her he was going to steal my car if I financed one and that he hated me. He called me names. He talked shit about me. I almost fell over because conversely he had told me how much he hated her!

I was gutted again. I couldn't fathom that he was in the game of gaslighting and I was the mark and he had a secret agenda after all. Dating me to use and abuse me knowing how raw I was from my past. He cut me deep. I thought he was my great hope. My hero. The one. This betrayal struck me like lightning. I gasped and ran barefoot down three flights of stairs and down the road through Gastown running and crying, barely able to breath.

He was calling my name as he chased me. Eventually he caught up, I pushed him and yelled at him to get away from me. He kept trying to console me and trying to hold me telling me he knew I was there and he was only saying those things to win her on his side again. In my head I was thinking, well what else is he going to say… I eventually calmed down. He insisted he was telling me the truth.

When we returned she was gone. I picked up my pipe and smoked my crystal meth and Down together. As usual my emotional cocktail did the trick. I felt like I was staying in something I knew wasn't right and I wasn't respecting myself because I should have held him accountable for so many things but I just couldn't. I liked that he was a bit younger than me and I was attracted to him. I am not a weak man, I demand respect from my partners, usually. When he struck me, it crippled me. The normal response to someone hitting me is anger, but I felt mass amounts of confusion and instant tears. I had marks all over my body, inside and out, that I had to hide in public. I remember telling my mom after one of our fights, I had blood on my face from a wound that he inflicted and she said to me, "why don't you hammer him back Jer, you're not weak, defend yourself." I thought about this conversation over and over again. The time that I finally snapped back at him was when we were fighting about something and I was walking down the street away from him. I could tell he was angry with me because I wasn't feeding into his anger. He came up from behind, grabbed the side of my face to try and turn me around, so he could hit me, so I used the momentum and finally snapped, I nailed him square in the nose.
I yelled, "Touch me again!". He covered his nose and grunted. I was furious. I just turned around, I knew I had blood leaking down my face from his nails

but I didn't care. He tried running after me, he said he was sorry but I just kept walking and he just kept following. Never mistake silence as weakness, or the fact that not reacting with instant aggression makes me a coward. I can hold my own, I just wasn't taught to hit the people I loved. Because I loved him and he was saying that he loved me, I felt like maybe this was a darker part of love, like the saying, "well you hurt the ones you love the most". There was major codependency between us and we were deep in trauma bonding, it didn't inspire self confidence.

When reflecting back over the past several years, I see that I should have left him earlier. I should have not let so many things happen with any of the men that I shared myself with. No matter what, not having my back as a partner is simply unacceptable. He should have told me he was going to trick her like this, make me a part of it, not talk about me behind my back the minute I left the room. If I didn't catch him, I am sure I wouldn't have been told about it. I also had lots of Down go missing in the place we shared. This friend of his didn't do Down, but he blamed her for everything that went missing of mine. There were times where my money would go missing and he wouldn't have any either, but suddenly he would be smoking Down. He was sneaky, drugs make people sneaky. All of this made me suspicious of his real intentions.

It is interesting when I reflect on Jason as a person, he didn't smoke Down when I met him. His integrity went downhill the more and more he used and I witnessed him become a completely different man. This realization is what allowed me to think, maybe he isn't all that bad, the drug just made him decline. Time will tell, I am a demonstration that once the drug is gone and sobriety is embraced, underneath it all a great man can stand. However I wonder how much responsibility the drug actually has for the character flaws that flare up during addiction. Being on drugs can be used as an excuse to an extent, I wonder if certain people try using it to excuse their awful behavior.

Every time my heart took a chance it was broken into tons of pieces and my mind was not running on all cylinders. Drugs made me allow behaviors that went against everything I stood for. Drugs do have the ability to demoralize someone. Drugs made me allow bad people to occupy space around me.

Jason fucked me around, like this, so many times. He was responsible for my arrest in North Surrey. I found out he cooperated and collaborated with the police when we both rented a U-Haul during the winter to live in because we were homeless and freezing. We were a couple days overdue with payment, when that happens they consider the U-Haul a stolen vehicle. I didn't know that. He got arrested and then sold me out instead of taking the blame like a man. I wasn't present when he was caught in the Costco parking lot in North Surrey. We had a fight while we were in Costco shopping so I left him and walked to the nearest gas station to do some drugs because I was so stressed out. When I returned to the parking lot where the U-Haul was parked, I happened to see a hooded figure quickly duck behind a nearby bench. He had a walkie talkie radio in his hand that was up against his mouth as he talked into it. I saw it in a split second. I knew exactly what was happening, so I instantly turned and quickly walked away from the lot, hoping to escape. I didn't know where Jason was, he wasn't responding to my texts or calls and we weren't doing anything illegal so I didn't think that it was odd that he wasn't replying. Little did I know he had already been arrested which is why he couldn't. An unmarked cop car swerved in front of the crosswalk as I was trying to escape but then three other officers came flying out of the bushes and I was done for. He is the reason I got all the charges. When I later plead guilty to the charges, my lawyer read me the police report which confirmed his actions. Jason was let out hours before I was, plus they let him sit in the cop car and wait for me to come back to the U-Haul, it was all premeditated. You don't do that to the person you say you love, especially in the criminal world, cooperating with the police is something people get killed for. In this dark side of the world, being a rat is the worst thing you can be. There were also countless times that I had to go to the emergency room and he would leave me there alone and disappear with his friend from Ontario, but anytime we went there for him, I was there the whole time from start to finish, I loved being the one who was there to support him. I wish he felt the same about me, that's all I honestly ever wanted from him, I just wanted him to love me like I loved him. But he knew how to play me, he knew what to say to me, how to pull at my heartstrings, how to make me doubt myself. My heart was really hurt and when I was arrested in January, I wrote him so many letters and got no response. In March he had a phone for a week and then went MIA again.

My family wrote to me the whole time while I was in jail, it's not hard. And if he truly loved me he would simply want to talk to me, so I can't keep making excuses for him anymore. It's hard because I felt codependent on him, I loved him, on the phone he said he loved me and was having the worst time without me. He missed me. However, he couldn't be bothered to write. He said he hated his Ontario friend, but anytime he wasn't with me, he was with her. His actions didn't match his words. I want a love who wants to talk to me. Who shows it. I can't be involved with him until I get myself together and healed.

He played a major role in my trauma and hurt. I feel that he will have to fix himself first, if he wants, before anything happens.

I still felt like I couldn't go on without him. In one of my sister's letters to me I told her how badly I was struggling, she said to me, fiancés don't cheat, steal or lie. I know this, even when I say it out loud, it sounds ridiculous to say. I can't imagine Jason telling me that she is wrong, fiancés do cheat and lie, sometimes they kick the shit out of you, sometimes they steal your shit… it's totally normal…! I just got high when I got hurt by him, this is why drugs were intertwined with my emotions.

I've always believed in the divine, a higher power. Through the last seven years of addiction, I was selfish and self serving. We are all selfish; addicts just are but I never let what love meant to me diminish in the fires of addiction.

Mentally and emotionally my life was completely unmanageable, obviously, I was needing my drugs to even move physically. The more I learned, the more I can now admit to everyone that I couldn't get sober with my own tool set, and that's okay. It's okay to need help, I struggle with admitting that. When I can help someone I feel great, so why rob someone else from this sensation? I have to be humble with this. My divine power, my spirit, my god, will restore me to sanity, I'll get my shit together if I finally admit to the reality of my addiction, that I am powerless.

I need to shed some light and validate the bad shit I did and investigate my moral inventory, my wrong doings. Sin. I felt I needed to get it out. I needed to tell someone, I needed and desired to be validated. In doing this I had to be honest with everyone. I did bad things, I hurt people, I disregarded proper community prosperity and insulted many institutions. I didn't and couldn't have the capacity to care about what was going on around me. I felt I was owed by the universe. Like I could take, because I was taken from. How could karma be so one sided? When you open up to someone and admit you're ready to do this, the divine God, your high power will remove all your character defects, I learned.

If I keep using drugs I will keep suffering from them and keep wearing all this trauma. It feels so heavy and suffocating which only triggers the crave of drugs. Following the steps in the AA book is my only hope to get rid of this. Using drugs to handle my trauma is something that I have been doing for years and look where it's gotten me.

There was a time during my addiction, when it started to get really bad, where I couldn't hide the fact that I was a drug addict because my looks started to deteriorate. Each time I made contact with my mom I could hear the hurt in her voice. Everytime she updated me on my family events, I would cry as soon as we hung up the phone.

Me, letting myself down, the shame, the dishonor, was so debilitating that I couldn't look in the mirror anymore. There was a long period of time that I couldn't look myself in the eye. I hated mirrors, which was very unlike me, but that was how aggressive my shame was. This is how I experienced and practiced repentance. I do believe that my god could and would humbly remove my shortcomings if I asked them to.

I needed to demolish my guilt and shame, they are poison and why I used drugs. I needed to apologize and seek amends with the people I hurt. For me, my family was huge. I wrote a thirty-two page handwritten amends letter, explaining everything I went through, all the words that went unsaid because they only knew from the outside looking in. I felt I owed them. I had to experience being vulnerable, uncomfortable, embarrassed and humiliated to actually admit my faults but most importantly I had to seek their love and support so that the little scared boy on the park bench felt the courage and bravery to look up at my hand and grab it, accepting the help.

I made the letter out to my mom, sisters, brothers, dad and step mother. All these beautiful humans were affected and had to watch in horror. During my addiction I couldn't keep any promises. They all tried to intervene at some point in their own way but I was too lost and rigid in my addiction, there was no way I could be helped. So I needed them all directly to know my truth.

For me, this letter needed to include my story of addiction but not in depth. I tried to keep it G-rated detailing the most important parts to help my family make sense of what my life looked like and what I went through. I explained my heart breaks, how it felt to be called worthless, useless and how much the abuse modified how I viewed myself and changed my every move. I had to imagine what it must have looked like from the outside looking in at me and their view point. So I would explain why I did and didn't do what they thought I should have done or shouldn't have done.

I educated them about the drug and the power it wields and the effect it has on the community and the user. What it means to be a junkie and how it truly feels. It detailed my sincere apologies for the damage I have caused them, the hurt that I burdened them with. All the tears that have been shed by them over me. The thought of that kills me inside, because that is the last thing I would ever want.

The purpose of it isn't to spark pity or make excuses for my behavior, that's not what recovery is about. My goal with my amends letter was to comfort their minds and to unburden them from confusion, frustration and to alleviate some pain they may have. I thought maybe if they finally knew how bad it was for me and all the things that happened behind the scenes then they would hate me less because perhaps they thought I was just out and about, getting high, loving my life, no matter what pain I was inflicting onto them and myself. I wanted them to realize that anyone that does Down or heroin hates it. It's the fuel to anyone's ride, to their inevitable undoing.

It took my strength away and replaced everything with this synthetic power which I needed because my engine didn't run naturally anymore. My scars cut so deep, my pain and heartbreak was so real. I didn't know how to handle all these fucked up feelings. I wrote this amends letter during my last stint in jail, I needed them to know I plan to actually stay sober and that this time it's real and I am ready. It finally clicked for me, I had my "aha!" moment.

The only great thing about imprisonment is being forced into sobriety. I am grateful for that now. Letting my little brothers down, my two beloved little boys I helped raise. Changed their diapers, watched them enter the world, promising to always be their older hero brother. I idolize them. They felt the same - about me. The feeling of knowing I was letting them down, having them think less of me, knowing maybe they were ashamed of me broke me in ways no one will understand. Perhaps they wished I wasn't their brother anymore. Did they hate me for what I have become? Did they feel abandoned and have scarred them, so that no matter what I do, it couldn't be healed?

Following that, my beautiful older sister, always so perfect and my genuinely, great mother. My darling younger sister, I didn't even get to see her grow up, I missed all her highschool years. I hate that. I abandoned her too. My dad and step mom tried to help when they were given the chance. I visited them one time during my addiction and I was severely Down sick. It was their first hand experience in just how powerful the drug was. My stepmom tried to give me pain killers, but I popped them like tic-tacs, they did nothing for me. My withdrawal was so aggressive, they just layed with me in horror and despair, seeing their son in that condition was devastating. They ended up driving me back downtown Vancouver to my drug dealer's house and gave me a little bit of money to get drugs and said whenever I was ready to accept help, they would be there in a heartbeat. I love them for trying. Whenever I was starving and homeless, my mom would call Panago pizza and order me a bunch of food and I would go pick it up at the nearest location downtown. My family is my kryptonite. My ultimate devastation. Internally fighting for my life in so many ways, knowing that no one can truly understand me unless they are exposed to what I was. Knowing nothing I can try to illustrate so it would help all of them to try to understand me.

I had already made peace with the fact that my family probably didn't accept me any more and they most certainly didn't trust me. I made mistakes, I took things without asking for permission. I didn't accept this version of me either.

At least we could relate to that but it is still a horrible reality in my mind. All I can do is speak my truth, find the words, and then they can have a proper picture of my life for the last couple years of my absences and why I was impossible to contact. Barely feeling like a person. So they would have more of an educated opinion of me. Maybe then they can see why I made mistakes, why I did stupid things, why they were affected, even though I tried so hard to shield them. They probably didn't know? I tried to make sure they didn't. I felt I couldn't possibly burden them with any more negative things.

But I've never needed their help more. This is pretty much life and death for me. I'd have to open up to them . Maybe they'll think I'm a loser. Maybe they'll wish I wasn't alive anymore. Maybe my siblings think I didn't care that I was hurting our parents.

My mom is my best friend and I am so protective of her. I literally have almost been killed trying to protect her. Constantly she was threatened by everyone who wanted to manipulate me because they knew she was my treasure. They tried pulling her in, calling her and trying to manipulate her against me. They threatened to hurt me if she didn't send money their way. I hate myself for putting her in danger, even though it wasn't me doing it, but simply because she was my mother made her a target in some ways. I HATED that. I always felt unequipped, waiting for someone to yell CUT because this was like a horrible movie and somehow I was the main character, clueless, stupidly loving the wolf dressed in sheepskin.

Think of your girlfriend or boyfriend who you love, imagine secretly they started doing the things I've shared. It's a mind fuck. A recipe for the most horribly perfect disaster. I was set up for failure because I wasn't taught to think like these horrible characters around me. Trying to process one atrocity at a time, living a life in fast forward.

The atmosphere always felt thick, always moving and if I stood still I got "clobbered "which is why I just kept moving from one heartbreak to another. I had proof that anyone who entered my life, at this point, isn't random; that there are no coincidences. This made my life stagnant. Colorless. My way of life is so mangled, surrounded by terribly broken people, everyone has a price and loyalty was easily bought, success became a dangerous thing. I started questioning and doubting my thought process.

I felt like I was powerless…useless. Maybe I would be better off dead. Then I wouldn't have to walk through my pathetic life. The things I've seen tormented me. People commit suicide, jump off seven story buildings in despair. I've talked to so many damaged people with crazy terrible stories but I loved hearing about them. Lots of druggies, deemed losers by society, I still felt honored that these people felt safe enough to share their inner demons.

There's so much more to the individual who are drug addicts. It's a choice technically, a wicked terrible choice but how they got there was always different and it made them the worst version of themself. The free choice to turn to drugs was heavily taxed and came with a terrible debt that demanded repayment. I'm not perfect. I made mistakes. I own my actions. I can't change the past, it's extremely hard to not live with regrets… with my history. My intentions were .to never hurt anyone, I failed this, I have regrets, I don't know how I could not.

I can only try and break down my events that led up to each hurt, to accept the reflection in the mirror. I miss my family. I miss myself. I understand why people say that addiction is a disease and we're sick. Sounds like an excuse but everything does. The minute I crack open my deeply buried boxes of emotions, I break down and cry. I feel so many shades of hate, hurt and depression. Everyone that knows me, knows I'm powerful and intelligent which goes to show, it could happen to anyone. I don't have a right to judge. It is important to really be educated before forming an opinion on anything or anyone.

I try to understand rather than "nail" a title or a judgment on them. The concept of confiding in a God felt complicated to me… How could I possibly confide in an entity I've never seen or heard not to mention with all the horrible realities I've been subject to. If there is a God, where is he? How is he allowing all this? How could you let this happen to me? How can I possibly find hope again, my fire, my shine has been taken away time after time. Letting evil steal my power.

What I would say to the people I love is:

"You're someone I trust, a word that has become scarce in my life. Some things are easier to write down and I feel I do owe you an explanation. I want to earn back your trust and your affection. You're so valid in your emotions. I understand if you're upset with me, know, I am upset with me too. I accept your every emotion and I am so sorry. I'm so sorry. And I know those words don't mean much anymore but I promise you with my whole heart and soul that I am very sorry and wish I was different. I wish I could go back. I have a disease, a mental illness. And that's not an excuse and I don't want it to be, but I do have something wrong with my brain and the way it perceives thoughts and emotions and rationality and decision making whenever I'm under the curse of drug addiction. When I think about it, it makes me want to scream and pull my hair out because I feel so out of control. Temptation knows it makes me vulnerable and weak. I just want to get the rush and high again because it's the only thing that brings me peace in the middle of all my shame, even though I know without a doubt it won't fix anything, just make it worse. That's the only comfortable decision I can make. I can't stand to even think about reality when I think about how I've lied to you, made you feel like an idiot for tricking you, it makes me despise myself. Just know that by me doing that to you and disappointing you is what pushed me over the edge to make the hard and uncomfortable decision to truly embrace sobriety and recovery this time in jail. I'm stuck right now, for me I know there is only one way back out. I have put myself in a place where there is no access to drugs and I am making it a positive environment that's solely for healing. I know how my mind works, a little bit at a time I remember how much better and full life is without chasing a high. My spirituality and relationship with God is real. He is good and I know how much he loves me. But that's just how powerful and deceiving the drugs are. It dominated my thoughts and emotions, and the lengths I take to get the drugs bring more shame that it just fuels the fire. This isn't going to be my life, I truly believe that. I know what my life looks like when I am not in addiction. I can't put my time and energy into anything else while I'm an addict because feeling that high is all I want. The feeling of being high feels so good, it's all I can do to get that feeling as often as possible because I have lost the natural ability to feel anything good for so long. That's why I feel like I have a disease or something is wrong with my mind. I don't like what I'm doing, I hate it while I'm doing it and when I'm not. I don't enjoy anything about it, it is literally like I am trapped. I feel like I can't stop chasing the escape, the high, I can't get myself to forget about it and to just live life as it was before chasing the high. It makes it impossible to mentally do anything but chase the high and get high. I don't know why but once the high is re-introduced, anything that doesn't have to with it is depressing and seems impossible to do without being completely miserable. All of what I'm telling couldn't be more accurate and true and I hope you believe me because the lies I tell you and hurt I have caused you is not from the real true person I am. Drugs have caused me to do things to myself and other people that make it hard for me to look at myself in the mirror. I never intended to hurt you, in fact I tried so hard, killed myself trying to prevent it. Everyday I find myself more and more. I want to clap my hands and poof! I'm all better. I just want everyone to accept it, accept me. I know I'm damaged goods. My road to recovery is intense. Experts say I'll have to work on it every day. They say my sobriety is a miracle, they say it's a matter of life and death. I don't want to rely on anything because I feel I was tricked in the past and had to rely on the smoke of death to get through the day. I'm learning. I'm working on my scars. I hope the people I love will feel comfortable opening up to me as I have to them. I have to make the first move. If you let me, I want to earn your trust and respect back, I want you to be able to depend on me again. It will be a journey. I respect whatever that will take to earn that back because I understand I've lost it through the years during my shitstorm. I'm not looking to make excuses, or to justify and claim my actions were okay, because I know they weren't.. It's unacceptable to me as well. I'm delicate, I'm still suffering, but I'm trying to untie this knot. I want to make this right. I'll need your support. You're unconditional love. I'm hurting. But I'm not taking the cowardly way out and doing drugs and getting high downtown Vancouver anymore. I'm taking it head on now, sober, searching for happiness. I love you. I miss you. I hope this finds you well, I'm not trying to scare you, I hope my intentions are clear here. It may be an overshare, but like I said, I feel like I owe you an explanation for my absence. I'm sorry for putting you through this if you felt dragged in the mud. Be comforted in the fact that this hasn't been a picnic for me either. I say this with a heavy heart and I'm extremely emotional. Being so lost, I'm comforted with the fact that I can be found. Before it's too late. All I can do is speak my truth and get my power back, you all are the lights in my sky forever shining bright. I refuse to be a stranger in each of your lives and you guys being a stranger in mine anymore. I love you."

I've imagined having this conversation with them so many times in my mind.

I realized that my amends letter was as much for me as it was for them. For me to be able to prepare myself to be open and honest with myself, I had to dive into my deepest hurts. Remind myself of all the tears I shed and why. It's extremely overwhelming and that feeling of being overwhelmed is what drove me away to use something, anything to make it stop hurting.

The reason that I was in so deep wasn't only because of the amount of drugs I was using, but the calamities I was trying to escape. The intimacy between me and my partners, the people that I fell in love with tore down their walls for me and I for them. I may have been uneducated in many dark things, but I am not a stupid man, I promise. The partners that I chose to give my heart to, are beautiful in their own way. They have their own stories, in the world we were in, they were taught not to emote, not to show their weaknesses because when they did, many years before I came into their lives, they were burned so many times. It's hard to not be jaded.

I walked into their lives, with them already having so many years of experience, and me with none. Now that I have had many years, I understand where the frost comes from and how it was produced. I can see how every time a heart breaks, the color of it changes darker and darker. This isn't the idea of being jaded, it is just simply the aftermath of breaking.

I can have all the understanding in the world, and all the positive attitudes at my disposal, but it's just the reality of what happens when you get your heart broken. I will love again. I love, love. I do think it is the most beautiful human connection that we as humans get to have that's free or so it should be.

When I think of the tender moments that I have shared with each man, we were so connected. We loved each other more than anything and I know with each man, I was something they haven't ever had. The things that I bring to a partner, how deeply I can love and truly, genuinely without conditions especially in the atmosphere of addiction, it rocked their world. They didn't know what to do or they were too scared to believe it was true because so many suitors before them didn't have pure intentions. I didn't know this, I didn't think that being addicted to a drug would change love languages or morals. This is why I was so badly beaten and bruised. I had to learn the hard truth.

I wish and hope that if I can try and teach something to addicts it is that you still do have choices. I understand how destructive it is having your pure and innocent heart broken and deceived. It's a lot easier to just shut off the emotions and not care.

I used fentanyl for years. The things that happened to me, I was in a place where hearts are thought of last, they are just collateral damage, the thing that everyone downtown is carrying around with them, is a broken heart. Fentanyl steals the attention of healing, it takes it and suppresses it making it unachievable. The only way to find it, is to finally hold your head up high, embrace courage, and lock eye contact with the damage, the depression, and don't look away.

Realize, you don't need anything to handle it, healing will come automatically if you seek it. It listens to your heart and your mind, but your mind can't think properly for as long as drugs are in the picture.

We humans are resilient, we have the abilities to handle everything within this human experience. Shame and guilt are driving factors and the very reasons I chose to use drugs was when I couldn't look in the mirror anymore because of everything I had done to the people I love, even if not directly, indirectly this hurt me even more.

Disappointing my family, but especially, my mother, shattered me. Perhaps my little brothers wished I wasn't their brother anymore or my parents regretted giving me life. My actions might not have been directly hurting my mother, but seeing her suffer and cry, was something I couldn't bare. My choices, my selfish choices, affected her so much and I was responsible for her nightmare. I couldn't believe that I innocently chose to love, and that got me in so much trouble all around.

I am no con artist, I am no liar, I am not someone who likes to hurt or disappoint anyone. My intentions were always pure, and yet I was eaten alive. I always knew in the back of my mind how devastated my mom and my family were, they tried to save me many times. They begged me to come home and to get help, the shame and guilt I carried was because I was too lost and afraid to admit to them what was truly happening in my life and what was happening to me.

The idea of making amends is to very clearly, very honestly, say all the things that have gone left unsaid. I wasn't in a place where I could take the time and explain to them the truth because I didn't really have the answers yet and because I knew even if I did, they would invite me to come home, and I would have to refuse because they wouldn't understand, it would be a disappointed and I couldn't take that on. I was fucked if I did and fucked if I didn't.

The reason making amends comes after many crucial steps is because I still didn't know how to explain it and I didn't yet have the tools and understanding to be able to make a proper amends. This step is so important because it is the guilt killer and shame breaker. My world got so much brighter when I forgave myself. I finally stood up tall and strong for the younger me that got hurt and abused, so badly petrified, and put my hand up with the stop motion. It is like a scene in a movie where the light of the good destroys the darkness of the bad, and all the monsters flee and they realize they don't have the power here anymore.

Now, I know what "sinning" does to me, how it makes me feel, so I will from now on be proactive and choose to act with integrity, trying my best to not hurt others. I need and feel very self aware of all my personal inventories. I talk out loud, meditate by writing to consciously contact my God, devine, as I understand him, always having an open mind and heart and always learning so I can carry this out. By doing all this, my spirit has reawakened. My light is shining again. I feel like I'm starting at zero again.

I need change, recovery, and healing. I don't want to be stuck in a loop, doing the same things day in and day out.

I want to avoid the situation where the minute I get out and get the chance to use I'll just get high, find Jason, remain abused and get my destructive agenda back in place. This would make me feel 50x worse because of letting my family down and all the ramifications that come with that. My guilt and shame will skyrocket and I'll be disappointed in myself again. I would need to continue to get money by committing crimes. Denials would continue and I know I would mess up with the court and I would be back in here again, not moving forward at all.

It would all be for nothing.

My fear of my family getting old and me missing out on their lives would eat at me, time will fly by and I will have nothing to show for myself. This is a major fear of mine. I always secretly thought of things, and I always wondered when and how God would present himself to me. I realized the sense of his presence had been blotted out by internal worldly clamors, mostly those within myself and because of this I didn't realize, it's always been there but I was blind.

Society has the mindset of *well it's a choice* he is making. I've learned that this is known as commonplace observations. This would be ignorance and misunderstanding. For anyone to understand they would have to be able to put themselves in my shoes and be an addict.

This choice reminds me of a time Kyle made me sit outside while he went to see an older man named Craig, who was a client of his, when he was an escort. We were together but he needed money so he made me wait outside in my car while he went inside to have sex for money. I was devastated. I was banging on all the windows and doors of the house begging him not to do it. Now imagine your partner doing this to you. This stuff doesn't happen to proper people in proper relationships. *Choice is a fickle thing.*

Choices have consequences, bad ones leave scars. One major scar that altered the way I looked at Jason was when he was angry with me over the fact that when I received my monthly payment from the government, I bought a phone and for some reason he didn't want me to. He fought with me on it, the whole way to London Drugs, and even after. He was so nasty to me regarding the phone, I tried to explain that we needed it to communicate with other people, to make things happen for us. I said we could use it and then return it in 14 days as per the return policy for phones. When I finally stood up for myself and said it is my money and I can do whatever I want with it technically. Jason spat on me and slapped me across the face in the middle of Georgia street, downtown Vancouver. How does one think spitting in someone's face is an acceptable choice of action? How could my standards be lowered so low to just wipe it off and just continue on like nothing happened. The biggest reason why it did major damage of me isn't the fact that spitting on someone is the most disgusting way to say "fuck you" to someone…it was because now I know that he is capable of this kind of behaviour. Now I know that in his mind, he can get to a place where he thinks that's acceptable to do to someone you love, or even just in general. Once an action like this, or being violent, or being unfaithful has been done…It makes a clear statement about that person's integrity and their own volition. It can't be undone. It can be forgiven, but it can't be reversed.

By doing recovery work and sharing my life with you, I really see things extremely differently, like a new shade. Drugs really lowered my standards of acceptable behavior towards myself. Growing up I broke up with an ex girlfriend, when I dated women, for being drunk and saying "fuck you" to me. I was 19. Back then I was so appalled. Now looking at what I've allowed, shame and embarrassment is tremendous, I really let myself down. How can I, as a child, have a higher standard than me, as an adult? It's backwards.

Drugs have that effect. I'm really starting to see things more clearly. As I reflect on everything that took place between me and Jason, I don't think he loves me, or maybe he just doesn't actually know how to show love. When we were living in that canary yellow SRO, there was a time that we had another huge fight. As far as I am concerned and for the record, you should never hurt your partner physically. There's never an excuse or reason to lay hands on someone you love in a physical way. That night we fought physically, but when people knocked on our door he would open it and act as if everything was fine, even though it sounded like we were killing each other. He tried to hang himself from the roof when I told him "this is fucked, I'm done, move out of my way".

I felt like someone took the air out of my lungs when I realized what he was trying to do. Obviously I stopped him and from that moment I knew he needed help. It was traumatizing, I saw just how troubled he was, which sparked the part of me that wants to help fix someone who is damaged. He maintained a very surface relationship with his mom, he didn't tell her how bad it was, that he was doing down and overdosing. He was suicidal. I couldn't leave him. So I stayed. I did tell her out of fear and that's when she told me he was bipolar, had issues with down back home in Ontario. He did over a year of jail time and currently had warrants back home.

Maybe this whole time he has been lying. Maybe he is a "Kyle" and has been using me from the start. But why then would he have proposed in front of his mom and family when they came to visit. Could someone commit evil to that extent or was there just something more at work … I tried to understand him rather than hate him for the things he had done to me. No matter what I loved him for his flaws.

Humans are capable of epic "satanic" actions. There was this other friend of mine, now deceased, his name was Brian. Big guy, super sweet but the minute he did crack, he was a monster. He stole from anyone, he took from the homeless which is a huge no. The homeless aren't supposed to steal from the homeless downtown. It's a known pact, but when someone is in deep active addiction, all of the morals go out the window. There's an SRO downtown called the "Murray". Lots of crime happens there, tons of criminals, drugs, murders etc. One night a new guy, I'm not going to say his name, was turning 30 at midnight and was getting a huge lump of money from his family, his trust fund. Brian got wind of this and in his drug induced state of mind did the unthinkable. Brian was in his addiction, deep. I was at my friend's house on the fourth floor and he never locked his door.

Apparently Brian and a group of boys killed this poor random new guy who was inheriting the money and I guess they didn't know what to do with the body. They knew the only door that was open would be my friend's door. We had left for about 20 minutes to go pick up dope and when we came back there was a dead guy on his couch, with blood everywhere.

My jaw dropped, we had both just entered, took our jackets off and turned around simultaneously and boom. There he was, dead. We froze for a good 30 seconds and we looked at each other in horror, stunned. We had no idea what had taken place, we would never involve ourselves in murdering an innocent person or any one for that matter..

I'll never forget that moment, time stood still. My friend was too terrified to call the police because he didn't want to be held responsible. He made me swear not to tell. Everyone in that SRO knew about the death of this guy, but acted like they didn't.

I walked out, my ears were ringing, I felt like throwing up. I was pale and shaking. Shock. As I went down the stairs to leave, I passed some other tenants and they glared and asked if it was okay, everyone seemed so unbothered.

The police weren't called for two weeks. Yes, my friend, let this boy's dead body sit and decay in his locked bathroom in his place for two weeks. When I found this out, I threw up. My friend filled me in with the details. He finally, due to the smell, called the police and they removed the body.

Brian was killed sometime later, for reasons I won't say , it's not my story. My point is, the effect that drugs have on addicts, some of these are worse than others…clearly. It's just scary that Brian could speak 11 languages, had a good family, was educated, but the moment he smoked crack he was taken over by the devil. One time, outside the Murray I got jumped by "natives". I had my new phone out so they came in hot to try to take it and I saw Brian a couple blocks away and I yelled for help. Brian jumped in a cab and destroyed these guys and got my phone back for me. He did take my bag, but it's not like he was all bad. It's really confusing. Drugs make people do different things.

Atrocities take place when drugs are involved , if drugs are in your life horrible things seem to happen. There was another time, when I went to the sea ports in downtown Vancouver with a friend to find something that was his, instead what we found was tragic and linked to the drug world. As we entered the heavy gates to the C-Can swung open with a thundering clank. We were both hesitant when we entered, the hairs on the back of my neck stood on end. I could have left but something urged me forward, it was like a whisper in the back of my mind that wouldn't let me turn away. Inside the walls of the C-Can were rusted and decaying. The air was stale, heavy with the scent of mildew and something else- something faint but unmistakable. The smell turned my stomach and set my nerves on edge. It was the scent of death. When the light crept in from the doors and I stepped in I could see four little beds at each corner of the metal room with shackles hanging down from them and attached to something that was on each bed. What was in the container was enough to freeze me in my tracks. There was a light bulb that hung in the middle that gently swung as if recently disturbed. Beneath the light, on each bed lay a naked body, they were young women. I stared at the lifeless forms, my eyes drawn to the dark. The smell was overpowering now, filling my nostrils with the sickly sweet stench of decay. It wasn't just the bodies that held my attention, on the floors were used needles that once hosted drugs around each bed. The walls of the C-Can were covered in something strange, something that made my skin crawl. It was blood. My breath got caught in my throat, my vision blurred and I stumbled back, my head spinning. I tried to shut my eyes to block this horrific sight but it was too late, what I saw couldn't escape my mind. I could barely process what my eyes were seeing. I turned around and ran out, my mind a shattered mess of fear and confusion. The echoes of what I witnessed haunted me for a long time, it still does when I think about it. Seeing this hit my soul.

I had seen this in movies, fictional movies, never did I think that it was real. I could only think that these girls were someone's daughters, sisters, mothers and friends. Disgusting. Repulsive. I thought that seeing the dead body in the Murray would be the peak of my surprises, but this one took over my mind. I knew that I couldn't do anything about it, I couldn't call the police, I was well aware that in these situations, the sex trade organization is so high up, I'd just go missing. We never spoke of it again.

This was a totally different kind of helplessness, one that I had never felt before. These are the things that I can't unknow, or unsee, forever engraved in my mind, the faces I will never forget and knowing that there will be more. The power of drugs. People making terrible choices or allowing terrible things, dehumanizing things. I am lucky, drugs didn't make me demonic, they just dulled my shine. Put me in auto pilot.

Everyone has different reactions to different drugs. Maybe it made Jason evil. It made Kyle a monster. I started to use Down when I had the low human "world-at-its-worst" shocked moments, like when I saw the C-Can that day... It's okay, I'll be able to pretend I didn't just see that, or experience it if I just smoke my pipe.

Getting sober meant changing my way of life, but being constantly high has been my comfort zone. The darkside of the world really fucked up my head.

Seeing the world in this light made me feel raw. The lack of knowing what people are capable of and do to each other. I never even knew that, at the start, any of this could happen, I was a fish out of water.

The change is never fast or clean cut. Parts of my past still follow me. Everyone downtown moves around like pinballs clinking and clanking around. All the unknown groups and organizations, street teams, undercover enforcement, sting operation, swat teams and secret societies. We are all being watched. I don't say this like a tweaker, the more I started to be aware of what was going on around me, the more I was able to observe these movements.

After I was approved for disability in Vancouver, my name showed up on CSO online and having issues with the law, I felt like someone's hand was being held 1 cm away from my face, in my personal bubble, never alone but not in a comforting way. Privacy? Not a chance. I signed that away, I felt like I was always being watched. I'd see the same faces through the week, following me or just always randomly being where I was. Observing me, investigating me.

I experimented with different crimes that I had learned through Kyle. During the period when I fell in love with Jason, after the Kyle break up, I was a very angry, devastated and a begrudging human. I felt very wronged but because I am intelligent, if I would use my ways for evil and crime I'd be successful.

I did things I'm not proud of, lots of fraud and profile theft, but never to friends or family and it had to be insured, for example credit card fraud so the person could claim it, and the bank nullified it. In my mind, this made it an innocent thing. I never did crimes where the person was stripped of their finances with no recovery. Something happened to me which is why that became my mantra. Kyle and I got a place from our "friend" Brittni, she is a dealer at Murray. She told us that one of her friends was moving out of her place so I paid her $4000 to move in, damage deposit, first and last month's rent. It was dirty, so I offered to clean it. I was just so happy to be off the street and I spent all my money to get it.

Kyle was scarce, I thought it was odd. I was told she could be trusted so I did. I got a $5000 best buy credit card so I got a big tv, laptop, air conditioner etc. Two weeks went by, I cleaned it and was super proud of myself and was getting settled in. To my surprise, suddenly a woman and a man entered "my" place and I said, "uh…hello can I help you?" Turns out, this is their place, it was an AirBNB, and Brittni's friend lied to me pretending it was hers to sublet. I was deceived.

That's why Kyle wasn't there, he knew it but didn't tell me, so I was out $4000. I never got that money back and someone had come by before that and stole all of my new things from Bestbuy. I got nailed like this all the time. I call this dirty fraud, I felt like a dumbass. And shame on all these people for abusing my uneducated mind and taking advantage of me. It's like stealing from a baby. I had a lot of resentment towards a lot of people, it made me really bitter. So I hit my pipe.

All these "secret societies", some are very self serving. What they all forget is when we are arrested and in jail, we talk. I found out so many crazy things. I heard tons of stories that are truly baffling. I don't understand how it's legal or acceptable. I can't help but feel like I want to know, it bothers me, I want someone to give me the straight answer of what's really going on, it affects my will to recover. Will they let me? It's like asking about the unknown, it gives me huge anxiety and an overwhelming feeling of something looming over me, it doesn't seem fair. Aren't we all entitled to our own privacy?

Being considered a criminal, my privacy seems stolen. Since when was this okay?

The reason I felt I lost my faith in God, which impeded recovery for me, is I've seen the world at its worst. The realistic, skeptical side of me made me think, reason says, God, higher power greater than myself isn't real because he has allowed all of this to happen. It's man made.

Until I read a certain part in my AA book and then it hit me.
"Who of us had loved something or someone? How much did these feelings, these loves, these worships, have to do with pure reason? Little or nothing. We saw at last". Things like this started to make the wheels turn in my head. The biggest reason that made me want to change my life was because everyone that I met during my addiction, as they were in theirs, those that I liked…those that I loved. The more time they spent in this life and the more time they spent doing drugs impacted who they were, each time I would see them they were in a far worse condition from when I saw them last on the streets, here and there. A life with drugs is a life of decline. It is a life with chaos. I did meet people on the streets whose company I enjoyed, some were like me. I could tell that they didn't belong on the streets, addicted to drugs but circumstances led them here, they ended up like me. Those are the ones that every time our paths would cross, they looked worse and worse, or I would hear that they died of an overdose, or were killed for other reasons. They became another statistic. There is no other alternative or no other destination that the life of crime and drugs will take us. It would only get worse. It always only got worse for everyone. I was trapped, I got more entangled with the wrong people, death was knocking on my doorstep.

The reality smacked me in the face. I've loved someone clearly so hard and reasoning would have said, leave. But I stayed, I had faith in love which made me believe and modify my life and behavior. Why should loving a higher power, that reasoning is against, be different and change my life for good? Why wouldn't anyone want to believe in that? I think my way of thinking is so negative, I don't believe I'm worthy of anything positive anymore for myself, so I subconsciously sabotage the reality.

I now can proudly and humbly say I do believe in a divine power, higher than myself. I do truly believe I was meant to help those deep in addiction and mental illness. I'm on disability for depression and anxiety. I was so dead alone when I went through my traumas. Drugs were my safety net. Like someone who smokes cigarettes and needs their nicotine when stressed, the same goes for the drug addict.

But drugs changed me. They change everyone. Morals become blurry, selflessness gone out the window and for me, depression and anxiety, drugs became my therapy, my cigarette.

Jail is a living hell and I look at it as my rock bottom. Society has deemed us, the addict, unsafe, a threat to the community and has put us in here, forced into sobriety. Well, the idea is to be sober. Drugs are present, and for the first three months my health wasn't good. I had four seizures, split my head open, and my cell looked like a crime scene. Withdrawal. The death of the addict, and rebirth of the sober. I had to tie my red sweater around my head to stop the blood from gushing out, I didn't get any medical help until hours later, I was near death when I was finally rushed to emergency.

For the last two months while I was in jail this last time, I got lots of mail from my family so I was writing a lot. I became a cleaner on the unit, then asked for a bible and then AA. That request made everything spark into a wildfire of recovery. I was finally given the tools to cope differently. To heal.

I couldn't have done it without being in jail, ironically because I wouldn't be able to read and write. It's given me the ability to heal and seek amends and reconnect with my family giving me my spiritual awakening and the ability to share my story now.

Recovery is life and death. I have moments where I crave using. I know I am good at making money criminally. I can feel it knocking on my door. The easy way. There comes a time though in everyone's life when they struggle to decide between what is right and what is easy.

I won't be surrounded by good people if I go back to that life. Hurt people. Sick people. Electronics are always getting hacked, stolen, all my accounts compromised. I couldn't do anything, I was surrounded by people that could hack my phone, just by being near them, they could mirror my phone and see everything I was doing. I had no privacy anywhere with anything. It made my identity and personal information an easy target.

So many times I felt violated, I wasn't safe anywhere, was so disrespected and was easy prey to trickery which didn't help my sense of security. I had no protection. As I think about my security being taken away, I reflect on the amount of insult. When I emerged from addiction and started self help programs, councillors, whom I opened up about everything that happened over the last half a decade while on drugs. I had never dealt with anything. I didn't realize how much emotional and mental abuse and destruction that had taken place.

The reason being sober or getting sober is so scary is I'm losing my synthetic shield. I was happy to have this shield at least. A part of me is thankful that I did have this to cope with because who knows what I would have done to escape if I didn't have this. Sooner or later though, after I realized how destructive it was and all the negative ramifications that came with it, I got to a place of needing something different to cope because Down wasn't doing the trick.

My mind and body are marvelous mechanisms, so using drugs is a paramount key in the certain damages that have taken place over time. Rehabilitation meant, I have to rehab my thinking, my go to shield, because I've been very comfortable using drugs for this purpose. All I had to do was smoke my pipe and poof, my anxiety and depression was under control, in the past. To me, my depression is so tremendous, for so many reasons. Having a sober mind is terrifying because I'm forced to think and feel, putting myself back in the moment of each hurt and especially my guilt and shame.

I break down and cry. No one wants to feel depressed and anxious, trembling with fear is not a happy or joyful way to operate. I was always looking for a way to mask this or run away because I didn't know how to handle that, or it. It's the easier, simpler way to handle all the emotions.

I was told I wasn't good enough, or I wasn't worthy of living happily and my goals didn't matter. I wasn't allowed to fly anymore. In fact my wings were stolen so even if I wanted to, someone had already taken them. My pure light was blown out. So not only did it seem easier to do drugs, my mind was so filled with the thought that recovery and a joyful life wasn't for me anymore, I had lost my ability to have this. Drugs laid this idea on me, thickly implanted.

I realized my drug use was really a symptom. When I started to house clean internally and do my personal inventory I had to get down to causes and conditions. Good, bad and ugly. If I'm being honest with myself, resentment was one of my main catapults. I felt my faith and the magic was nullified. I was spiritually diseased, not only have I been mentally and physically ill, I was also spiritually sick. My self esteem, financial well being, ambitions and personal relationships (sexual as well) were damaged. I am sore and feel so burned up.

To have faith returned meant I could get my courage back. I have been tempted to do drugs by other inmates. Some of my inmate "friends" would come into my cell and give me empty sugar packs that they had put Down inside. They were doing it to be nice and they didn't know I was in recovery. I thought he was just giving me a sugar pack for my morning cereal, so I took it but when I realized what it was. I put it on my desk and stared at it. I have my "AA" book on the desk along with all the pages of my book that I have been writing while I have been in here, they all whispered to me, giving me a look of disappointment.

I don't want to lose my days sober. I am proud to say I flushed the sugar packet after he left. Go Jer!. The little Jer, on the bench in the abyss that I described earlier, feels hope when I do something positive and constructive, like this.

After all the trauma and that little guy being so violated, his anger has passed because of all the work that I've been doing, the healing work. I know that each person that has hurt me truly is spiritually sick. If I can't forgive them then I can't forgive myself. If I can't forgive myself then surely I can't expect or hope for others to forgive me.

I can't be a hypocrite and I know Kyle and Jason are deep in their addiction journey. And they've shared with me their past, so I can say with confidence that they have major trauma. My "but I can fix them" stripe definitely flared up and I had given my whole self to these people. I set myself on fire to keep them warm. I haven't loved and put myself first or been put first before my partners in years, or ever.

I can't be with them anymore. Jason, is breaking my heart. I know he's hurting, he hates Down, he's got a loving family. I want him to be well. I know if I get released tomorrow, if I were to go downtown and be with him, I'll relapse and I'll stay with him and continue to do drugs. It's happened before. I'll lose all my progress. I'll go to RACC, get my prescriptions for methadone and hydromorphone to sell for Down on Main Street and Hastings, my daily routine. I'll find out Jason cheated or was on grindr (the same as all the other times I was in jail). I would wait for a reply to my twenty plus long love letters that never arrived.

Even if his phone got disconnected, he knows he can go to the public Vancouver library downtown, for free, and message my mom on Facebook to connect, like he had in the past, but I got nothing this time.

My sister who is very much into healing and spirituality said to me that I deserved better, very simply. I whined and defended him and made excuses for his behavior. I love him but if I allow him around the little Jer on the bench that has finally lifted his head and is grabbing my adult hand finally willing to trust would flicker away again. Jason has really badly hurt that little Jer, so intimate and delicate. Jason will spook the little Jer off and the hope would fade away again. I have to put myself first. Once I have that little Jer on my back laughing and all healed up in recovery, then maybe I can cross paths with Jason again. Right now, Jason would threaten my recovery because he is very spiritually ill. He needs sobriety. Every addict does.

Doing drugs isn't a way of life, but addiction is a bitch. A stone cold heartless bitch. And for me, the bitch is dead. Even at my lowest lows, I have always felt I was meant for something special, something bigger. I remember one of my lowest lows, I got released from jail and Jason was broke, we were homeless and super Down sick. I went on his phone and saw that he downloaded grindr, I was devastated. He didn't even console me or feel bad. He would wait for his phone to die and then give it to me to look at. I was so cold, to the bone, it was winter and I was homeless. Cops took everything of mine so I had nothing, I was about 120 lbs soaking wet and I felt so defeated. I called my mom bawling. I hadn't talked to her for months, I said all muffled and distraught, "mom… im .. im…so so ..cold and ssss…starving." It killed her. It killed me.

We stayed downtown at this nightly shelter that's free, open from 9pm-5am only for sleeping. They make you sit on this bench in the lobby to see if you can sit up on your own, and I kept collapsing on Jason. Bless his cruel heart, he held me up at least. I could feel the beat of his heart, trying so hard, to make sure we got in. That was one of the worst nights of my life. I could barely walk, going through the hell of withdrawal, hating my life and thinking like what the fuck, how did I get here? How could I let myself get here? My poor mom.

It's times like this that made me think Jason isn't all bad. He could be just an opportunist and because I opened my heart to him it gave him every opportunity. I think his negative outbursts made it evident that he was suffering and an addict. I believe he is just as stuck as I am, he hates his life just as much as I hate mine and I am just collateral damage to him. I know it's difficult to be a good partner to someone when in addiction, I know the symptoms of addiction are of course selfishness. Not many have the capacity to be selfless while being an addict.

This is the first time I realized that love isn't enough. They say that love trumps all and before all of this I would have lived by those words. In my case, I can't let love trump my recovery, sobriety and spirituality because it would be a huge threat. I love very hard.

The way I love hasn't been working for me or my life if I'm being rigorously honest with myself. Love has to take a seat and not be the leading lady. I think that's why God made it so we are away from each other and have had no contact. That's the only reason my recovery is flowing, or blooming, that's the only way I am successful. I'm going to be real with you, my rights and freedom had to be physically taken away from me or the number of days or sober, that I have now, wouldn't be possible.

My higher power, the divine universe is telling me it's time to get your shit together. It's saying you're 31 now and before all this you aspired to be famous. I had looked into course work to get certified in life coaching and counseling in Vancouver, and then shit hit the fan: seven years of hell.

Maybe I had to go through homelessness, witness and experience the traumatic exposures I endured so that I can use all my wisdom and valuable life experience to be of service to others in this life. I know, I feel it in my bones, that I'm meant to do something special in this life. I have a passion for learning about mental illness, depression and anxiety, as I have been technically diagnosed with them.

I still feel there's no right way to work recovery because everyone's addiction is unique to them, everybody reacts differently to all drugs. Also, everyone's reason for using drugs is different. It depends what type of healing needs to be done. When I was arrested it was a blessing in disguise this time. If I can find a silver lining in jail, as I've been stripped of everything, then anyone can find their silver lining in a bad situation if they want to find it. It all depends how much you really want it.

In the bible it says, if you knock, Jesus will hear you and open the door, if you seek, it can be sought. I find that all the major institutions of recovery or any big life changing proceedings, they all have the same message but are just worded differently or the languages are not the same.

In my research, I have tried to keep an open mind to everything and everyone because no matter what, success is success. If anyone is successful in addiction recovery or any sort of mental healing with emotions then I want to hear from them because they must have done something right. For me, when I was hurting and in my addiction, any "professional" person that tried to assist me, that couldn't relate exactly to what I've been through, wasn't worth listening to. I want it to be relevant especially for anyone that went through the illegal criminal victimization that I did in the beginning. I want to be the cautionary tale.

So many people have their stories untold, especially if they have a criminal record. I have one now. Yes, I'm very distraught about it. I hope to expunge it, and look at what I'm doing. Should my credibility be nullified because of my crimes? Do all these words mean nothing? If anything they should mean more.

Silence speaks volumes and I will not be silenced. I've specialized in this area of life. I love singing, acting and writing. Authoring a book is my way to creatively "get it out". I hope it's a beacon for other people at any point of their journey.

One thing I'm struggling with is my embarrassment of the damage to my character that took place while I was battling addiction and depression. The "old" me. I worry about other people's acceptance of the "new" me. I used to, when I was homeless, ride around on the Vancouver public bus or sky station and sleep. Embarrassing. I'd ride around all day, especially when it was cold because all the homeless have to get warm somewhere. I dealt with mean workers sometimes, police and citizens being cruel like I had nothing and was so sick, couldn't barely breathe or move. I was hopeless and with no motivation and desperate for drugs and sleep. It was too dangerous to sleep on Hastings because at different times when individuals are really weak, certain evil people target others in that condition, they are an easy robbery.

I remember carrying Jason, because I was the "hustler" guy making the money. He was from Ontario so he didn't have the connections I had, but he drained me. It's extremely hard to get any ball moving when I had him laying in the way. I was suffering. Society has seen me at my worst. I was that homeless drug addict, on the street, looking like I'm almost dead, barely 100lbs, clothes wrecked, a hot mess, and I use the word hot very lightly. I was so defeated. I lost the will to live. I felt dead inside.

At the time I accepted that I would never have the platform to help anyone else. I would never get my things back like my identity, or my drivers license, a car, a bank account, a phone number or a place ever again. I had swallowed the defeated pill. I drank the kool-aid of defeat.

The grief of believing that I had lost my beloved family and my foundations, my facilities were burnt down. I was that guy laying on the street downtown that was near death, many times. The one you randomly make eye contact with, the piercing hazel eyes full of hurt, devastation, filled with fear and regret and self loathing. But they had a glimmer some unique special quality.

I was that homeless guy that you thought about and wondered how he got there. You wanted to know his story because he didn't seem like he belonged.

I decided to turn shame and embarrassment into power. As deep as it was wrong, as high as I was, I will and I want to make it right. I want to pay it forward. I'm practicing loving myself and forgiving myself. I was at my very worst. As bad as my situation was, how incredible would it be for anyone that was, how incredible would it be for anyone that may have seen me or known me back then, to who I am now. That feeling makes me hold my head high, with honor.

My mistakes don't define me and my past isn't any indication of what my future will be. This is my comfort. I can't change my past. Regret is like shooting myself in the foot, so I don't practice regret, I'm using my past as fuel for my future. I was ill, drug addiction is a disease. I firmly believe this and the idea helps me to deal with myself less harshly.. It helps me cope with any negative judgments that anyone may have.

One of my big questions or concerns I now have is: now that I'm very spiritually open and seeking a close relationship with God, or a higher power greater than myself … Where is he?.... I have figured it out.

In the movie "Transformers", Bumble-bee can't talk like the others so he has to use different clips of songs and radio broadcasts to form complete sentences or say different things. God is like that. He uses commercials, radio and certain people around me saying certain things or only hearing little snippets of conversations around me, things that pop up on my phone or news channels you see. That is my higher power trying to communicate with me.

Like when I ran out of ink the other day in here and I wasn't in the writing mood anymore. I told another inmate and he gave me another working pen and on it was written "You're business. New heights". This is a sign. Being open to God means being open to seeing when these things pop up. I have to be aware, patient and with my eyes wide open. I really want to observe and listen to everyone and to everything around me.

God, however you imagine him, can't speak sentences to humans directly so he has to use other tools and methods to talk to us. To have a relationship with him I need to learn this universal language he speaks. Everything happens for a reason and I firmly am not just saying that, like I always have in the past: I'm living it.

I will go for "sentencing" tomorrow. I hope to get released and court ordered to my mom's house with my little brothers and older sister ,which will be wonderful for me. I've reconnected with my entire family now, I talked to my mom and little brother Jackson on the phone and dad Lee. My sister Jaymie and I write back and forth all the time. I miss little Katie, and my other brothers.

Instead of heading back to my place right downtown Vancouver, I feel like I should go to Langley with them. I may feel strong here while I'm in jail but I'm restricted here. I need to remember it is by force. I know what it's like to be released in the past: I've rushed downtown Vancouver instantly to get high and see my love, Jason. I've been arrested multiple times. I've promised the court and my family that I was changed but in my head I knew I wasn't being real. If history has a say, every time I've been given freedom, I've ended up back here back to the life I know and have been living.

I've wasted too many years and it's gotten progressively worse each time I get more lost, each time putting myself in more danger and each time nearly getting myself killed many times. This is the first time I'm really taking my mom and dads advice. It clicked for me while I was here this time. AA/NA and bible studies have been a huge spiritual help to heal me. It's something I can't learn enough of, it's been a catalyst for me and changed my life. *God will help me with this battle, but I know I have to bring the fight.*

In the depths of my despair and hopeless lifeless states, I believe now it has enhanced me to be of service to so many different emotional elements. I don't know how I will do it yet, but I'm open to all possible avenues.

I know how hard the fight is especially when being burdened with clinical anxiety and depression. Addiction makes these mental illnesses severely worse. Getting sober is possible. I really want to live now, I want to work but working doing something that makes me feel alive as opposed to the rigid eat, sleep, work repeat lifestyle that really saddens me.

Time is cruel, it only takes, it never gives. We are all fighting the hands of time from the time we are born. I'm wiser and more aware now, I think I had to endure all the horror so that I can maximize what the divine higher power has instore for me.

Before, I wasn't open minded enough nor did my addiction let me even be able to have an open mind. My spirituality wasn't mature enough. Now I feel like it is.

It's hard because everytime I would get my hopes up and get to my feet, I've been knocked down in the past. I lived on Haro Street by myself for a moment when it got bad with that older gentleman, so I went somewhere else before I met Jason. I had it all furnished, I was arrested for 8 days and I came back to find out the keys had been changed and someone else living there. All my stuff was gone, again. Now I'm seeing that it was the universe telling me that it wasn't the right place for me, I just couldn't see it at the time. Today I realized that to be successful in my recovery, I have to do it alone. I have to let go of the people that were in my prior life. I finally understand when people say "if you love someone, sometimes that means letting them go."

I have to do that with Jason, or the Jason that was in my life. I broke up with him in a letter, cried, but said that I forgive him for all the hurt as I know he's deep in his own journey and addiction, and I love him and wish him well. I don't think he's abusive by nature. I've seen him cry, we have seen each other at our worst and most vulnerable. Perhaps we will meet again, both recovered and happily off drugs. I pray he does as well.

This is the first time I'm leading with my head, not my heart. And I'm putting myself first even though I'm fighting every fiber of my being. I just know his life has only gotten worse and if I go back, I'll be right back there, where I started. I do really forgive, but I won't forget.

I don't want to be with a person who has all this baggage, I want someone to fly with, not to have them on my back or vice versa. I want that epic love, pure, unconditional and actual caring about me, someone who can love like me.

It's not hard. That all consuming, can't live without each other kind of love. To be independently so dependent on each other, loving, living epically beside each other. I don't want to be treated like shit, I don't want to be shared or share and I want someone who has the capacity to feel this way too. For so long, I've compromised everything I believe in due to drugs and addiction, being sick spiritually. If I allow myself to be available and openly healed then that person can find me ,but if I return back to my life that I've been living, that won't happen. It comes down to common sense and comparing, using the tool of reason with my choices now. Its fucking painful to think I may never see the man I love again, or feel his lips again. Believe me, super painful as he is all I've known for years, good and bad.

I know I can't save him, he has to want to, that's the shitty thing when dealing with an addict... they have to want to change. I have mixed emotions when I think back and recall how dysfunctional and unmanageable my life was. I spent the last two years trying to find Jason all around town. Me and him were always looking for each other, never having phones. We got into lots of trouble because of this. One time, he went to a safe injection site by the Murray SRO downtown Vancouver, looking for me. He fell asleep in the portable that my manager friend ran. I finally was told he was there, as I ran down the back alley to the hut I heard him scream.

I forced myself in the door and I saw 6 guys in there and Jason standing on the couch surrounding him. I went ape shit and hit them, nobody knew that it was me. I grabbed Jason by the hand and yanked him out and we ran.

Birthdays and holidays were treated like just another regular day because of addiction, the magic was taken away. I couldn't get myself to many family Christmases. Birthdays, I have spent in jail which sucked. I have never had a successful celebration of New Years. Last year Jason was bear maced by guys from the Granville SRO because they wanted my drugs.

I know life is extremely difficult living downtown Vancouver when you're deep in addiction, but it really does hurt me that no one ever thought of me and wanted to make it special for me, I know sometimes it's literally impossible. I think, well I know, when your loved partner doesn't have your back or lets you down… it is a different kind of hurt and disappointment. I think it's so sad when two people were at one point madly in love and in the end they hate each other. I think that wasted love is a tragedy, due to miscommunication and addiction, a calamity. Drugs and money can make people do stupid things, it changes people.

Life as a drug addict is very dangerous. Lots of crime, lots of death and lots of very hurt and angry individuals. I got followed by people that would wait for me to be vulnerable or not looking and attack and rob me all the time, and people are aggressive and vicious, and I never knew who someone really was, couldn't trust anyone. I've never felt so united with everyone around me that played the game, but I was still severely….deadly alone.

Nothing was supposed to go differently because the divine universal rhythm is already set in place, we all are living it. This helps me with having no regrets. Even being heartbroken time after time and stabbed in the back too many times to count. I know my epic love is out there waiting for me to be ready for it when I'm deemed ready.

I found that in jail the guards and other inmates all reacted differently to the fact that I graduated with honors and have a good family, worked since I was 13, traveled to two different countries with work visas. Some wanted to fight me, thinking I had it "easy". Truth is, it was quite the opposite. It is remarkable what steps 4-8 in the big book can accomplish when dealing with all traumas. I believe addiction is truly a most severe symptom of trauma. I imagine when something traumatic happens it's like a seed being planted, what grows from it depends on how the person handles it and their atmosphere and the people that surround the environment.

I imagine the branches that grow are the symptoms like addiction and drugs. The reason the therapist or counselor is so important is because they allow you an outlet. Step 4-8 in "AA" consists of searching a fearless moral inventory of oneself, admitting to God, ourselves and another person of our wrongs, have God remove our sins, make a list of all the people you've harmed and make amends. All these describe the nature of addiction life coaching, and they work.

This time while I have been in jail, I've decided to get off methadone from 200ml, now I'm at 5ml so I'm feeling like shit. I've just been told about the new "sublicate" injection that you get shot in the tummy and it's good for a month. You don't have to use it daily and it slowly wears down throughout the month and you don't experience withdrawal. I'm definitely feeling it right now and I just keep telling myself it will be worth it.

I can see myself being in the Ministry of Addiction and Recovery Narcotics Unit for the government or something similar. I want a platform to make a difference in the world and to be a voice for those who are not able to speak up, are judged and ridiculed for being in addiction or recovery. I want to help them as I understand both sides of the downtown Vancouver drug addict and homeless calamity. I want people as well to understand the society side that looks down on the homeless and addicts for multiple reasons.

Perhaps it's going to be my responsibility to be that bridge to educate the "muggle" citizens about the drug addict "problem" and homeless issue/crisis. I bring an element of validity and relativism as I once was myself in the same position, I can speak from experience, the inside track. I can also help people get educated in recovery or get them help. Using my knowledge to educate a brother or a sister of a drug addict or criminal because I've experienced jail as well.

I'm not sure what my role will be. I'm not sure if I would give back to the world by working with the police to stop crime. Since I've done jail time, I've met so many different criminals and heard so many seriously crazy stories of every type. I've met men that have killed people, huge thefts of every kind, all aspects of drug dealing, dove into the sex trade, weapon sales, frauds of every type and so much more. There are the worst inmates, the ones that either abuse or rape women or underage persons. You don't see them for very long in the unit, because as soon as other inmates find out, and they do quickly, they get attacked and are often killed in jail. If I didn't know right away I would sometimes have conversations with them, regretfully.

One of the only positive elements about jail for me, is connecting with other inmates of all diversities and seeing how their minds are wired by just listening to them and having them open up to me so I could hear their story. I find the stories fascinating.

I had the shit kicked out of me by the police and treated like crap, like second or third class citizens … I feel like I'd rather assist by helping the very altered or corrupted, ill, criminals with getting their lives back by getting them off drugs, or show them they can live a happy sober life away from breaking any laws.

Often, when someone becomes a drug addict and ends up a downtown Vancouver homeless person, like I did, crime is a symptom of the illness. I know this. I never thought I'd ever break the law.
Looking back now, when I think about Luke, Kyle and Jason, I see that all the hell they put me through was because they were heavily addicted to Down and I didn't know how much power the drug wielded. Kyle fell in love with me when I think he wasn't supposed to. I think I was just a mark who he had set out to use and abuse, but then he started having feelings for me but that wasn't part of the plan. I understand the desperation of needing Down. I did things I never thought I would, many errors in judgment that I'm not proud of so I get why he did everything, it does not make it right, but I can relate to and grasp the concept. However, even in my deepest of addiction

moments, I never betrayed love or the love I shared with people, I never demoralized myself. Drugs really do have the power to make someone dance with the devil and make someone tap into their evil side. I may have become someone I didn't know and did things that were unthinkable, however, having my mother has always been my north star. I'd never let anyone do anything to her. When I was living at that older man's house, my morals and how much hold the drug had over me was put to the test.

Under a rug in his apartment I found a yellow temporary drivers license in my name, with my moms address. My email address was taken over, it was during COVID. I know I didn't go into ICBC and get my temporary license renewed, which means someone else did. I got into an online battle with someone trying to get my email back, I still don't know who it was. I had the primary phone number but someone stole my phone days prior to this, which means they had the primary device.

I battled with the unknown individual who had stolen part of my identity. We kicked each other off "my" account, having a change the password battle, but I knew all my past passwords so Google finally believed me and I gained access to my email again. I found corresponding emails, back and forth, they were getting a property appraisal and had me listed as the homeowner somehow of my mother's multi-million dollar home. It was at the time of Covid and because of this they offered to do a virtual tour and sale…the fraudster was impersonating me. When I realized what they were trying to achieve I was stunned. They were nearly successful at either selling the home altogether or trying to get an equity lean loan for half a million dollars. I was disgusted. I called the agent right away before the equity loan was approved, claiming fraud immediately.

The major fraudster that introduced me to Kyle, I remember him telling me that he had tricked a man named Ted by selling his mother's condo in Tsawwassen, for hundreds of thousands of dollars so I was well aware of the sinister people at work here. No matter how damaged and broken my addiction made me, I'd rather be dead on the side of the road than ever do that to my mother and brothers, but I can understand the temptation addiction desperately can accomplish.

What was a devastating factor for me, was that the older man must have been a part of it, because I found my driver's license in his house which possibly indicated that whoever committed this crime on me, was someone he knew. I would never betray my family like this, my mother did something right raising me because I wouldn't do anything against the family ,especially her. The power drugs have over a drug addict is magnificent and most "druggies" would have caved, selling out their family.

My mother is the most remarkable human I've ever known, she is what every mother should aspire to be. I've seen her in every light, she's been my hero, she's made mistakes, she's shown me that it's okay to be human, unapologetically.

I've been haunted for so long, no ghost is ever free until it's let go. I'm letting my old self go, with grace and tolerance. What my mother doesn't know, is all I've ever wanted was to be like her. She's wired me ever so carefully, crafted with unconditional love and respect. Even in my darkest hour, my loneliest times, that very traumatized little Jer crying on that bench amidst the monsters... he/I never stopped missing her. She never gave up on me even when I gave up on myself and she's never judged me even when I have given her every reason to do so. In life she is my guide post for everything.

Jail time during COVID was hell. I wasn't allowed to leave my cell for 22 days and had no communication, no TV, heavy withdrawal, no people and no writing. Nothing. I've only ever felt dehumanized one other time like this in my life. I wanted to peel my own skin off in jail and truly all I really wanted was my mommy.

Something I so often cried about was how much I missed my bestfriend and it killed me knowing how much she was missing me. If she ever knew what these monsters have done to her little boy over the past couple years, she would be mortified. I wanted to call her for help after each awful thing happened to me but I just couldn't put her through it. I know how devastated she would be to hear that I had gone through each situation and there was nothing she could do about it, I didn't want to do that to her so I just suffered alone and did more drugs.

When they finally took me off covid protocol and I got to call her, I bawled. I was barely able to muster words out, just the sound of her voice, sometimes I thought I would never hear it again. I've given her every reason to doubt me, I've made many errors in judgment, hit serious rock bottom and sunk my own ship to the deepest depths. She has always been idly standing by waiting to throw me a life raft. Her undying faith and motherly duty towards her children is my aspiration and has set my standard for any "bond" with another human at a very high level. Her heart is pure. Her mind is as straight and accurate as a cupid's arrow. Perhaps that's why a part of me was always aware that the person I was in the past 7 years wasn't really me. Far from. All of this respect and love, for my mom, added to my pain during my addiction.

I didn't have a constructive outlet to heal all my pain and suffering. Ironically, it took forced sobriety, reading the Big Book of AA and NA with bible study was to get another option, a better way, the solution to my salvation. I know the addict has to be ready and willing and I can only speak my truth. What worked for me, might not work for others but if anyone were to seek, it can be found. As I did.

The community outreach worker in jail came to see me this afternoon in my cell, he helped me call my landlord from the SRO I was last living at before being arrested this time. After discussing my rental situation I told them I wanted to cancel it, I wasn't going to be returning, I asked about Jason, he has a place there in my old SRO too and he told me that he was arrested back in March. My heart is finding some solace as the reason he isn't responding was because he wasn't able to. I am conflicted.

I made peace with the idea of Jason not being in my future. I assumed his silence was his lack of caring. When I was arrested previously though, we were in the same position and he never once wrote to me while I was in jail.

So I sent him a letter which he will get in the unit he is in, soon. I said now my heart is back in its place and properly protected again, in my right mind, reflecting back, we had high tides and lows. I don't know if he truly loves me, I think I do know, but me and him also know that the pure heart is easily fooled and defenseless and I've been severely deceived in the past. I told him to think hard before he responds because I'm stronger and wiser now, I wont be used, cheated on, lied to or stolen from, my standards are intact again.

Now I know that a person in addiction can do despicable things which is why I can forgive our past, but if he intends to continue doing drugs and isn't ready for sobriety and recovery then, please, let me go.

I can't imagine what it would be like for my mother to finally, after seven years of hell and her losing her son, her best friend, and knowing she can't do anything to help me, deep in my addiction, having to watch in horror would be incredibly tough. She's been waiting for me to finally get to this point. To change. She doesn't want anyone to interfere, I am almost there.

I didn't think I could ever break my own heart letting love go. For the first time love isn't enough to stay or return to him and the life we were living. For the first time I'm putting myself, my recovery, sobriety, before another lover. It's about progress not perfection.

If Jason isn't ready to heal and recover, then I know I have to eliminate him from my life, I hold no resentment and do not take it personally. I know more than anyone that a man in addiction is ill and is a modified version of themself, with a very corrupt mental and emotional state.

I can't let anyone jeopardize my recovery and wicked sobriety. One wise person once told me that, yes the idea of a broken heart is the last thing someone wants to go through, however, if you stay in an abusive or negative situation with a negative person, then you aren't able to be available when the right one comes, and it will. It's taken a long time to get to this level of understanding.

The withdrawal I am experiencing right now is killing me. I took my last dose of methadone this morning. I want to peel my eyes out, I can see why people keep using drugs right about now. I'm in so much pain and keep yawning, twitching, stretching all the time like my skeleton can't fit properly in my skin in so many ways. I'm irritable, I can't get comfortable, I can't sleep.

Sometimes, because I'm so adaptable, I forget how horrible being in jail is. I have court tomorrow. I got mail from Jason's mom, the records department here in jail intercepted it for some reason so I wasn't able to see what it was. An inmate isn't allowed to request information from any employee guard here, they are forbidden to relay any information. Luckily, I'm in good standing here in the jail. I've made some connections with certain guards, and I was able to discover that Jason is in here but on a different unit. This whole time, we could have been communicating instead of me being heart broken, thinking he was ignoring me and imagining the worst scenarios.

I got another guard that works in his unit, to give him a message for me. I don't know why he hasn't written to me this whole time, but due to timing,

I'm not going to hear from him before I get released. I still have no idea what his plan is.

I'm excited by the idea of getting to go home to my mom's. It will be hard adjusting, being homeless for so long it will be different. Being on Hastings street, I had to trust transit buses or skytrains to sleep, I would just go around and around the city never getting off. Sometimes me and Jason would be on for all day. We had no money, so I had to depend on St Paul's Hospital for food, and bagged lunches at RACC (rapid access addictions clinic). All the homeless people know what 24hr stores were open and where each of them are, especially in winter. Pretending to shop, just to be in the heat.

When I was homeless, I had to use whatever the city could offer citizens, many used the emergency room, lots used transit. Everyone knows the hours of operations, at night, I'd have to be careful because the last skytrain stops at New Westminster overnight and ends. The other one is the airport YVR, and I'd have to wait for hours for either one for the night buses. If I had a warrant, there's always police waiting at either end to arrest, they know that homeless criminals would be easy to find.

We would wake up and all of our belongings would be taken, pipes and drugs fallen on the ground for everyone to see, because we would fall asleep with it in our hands. Homeless people were an easy target for most, everyone knows that we would eventually have to fall asleep, being followed around town like prey, as the hunter awaits the vulnerable opportunity to strike in the moment of "homeless weakness".

It's a major contradiction when normal people think the homeless have it easy or they are lazy because they are jobless. Ironically I'd take a normal job over hustling in Hastings hell anyday. Eventually, when one regains normal mentality and is able to humanize oneself again. I must choose between what is easy and what is right for me.

I've come to the end of my jail recovery timeline, I'm out in the morning. I hope they allow me to return to my mom's. I've changed my place of residence there instead of returning downtown to my SRO. I also hope they don't give me more time but if they do, I wish that they allow me to serve my time in the community. For the first time, in a long time I honestly feel I'm ready, sober and want to be with my family.

I feel very strong about it. I feel humble, tolerant, selfless and continue to practice patience daily. I trust in my moms advice, sometimes I forget that they were once my age. It's taken me 30 years to mature and realize they, my mom and dad, actually know what they are talking about. Their advice and input are key.

In the AA book, there's a section that's "to the wives" and it states to remember the addict is extremely sensitive and in tune with all the desires from the loved ones. It advises the wives to not criticize or remind the addicts of lost time, and shame or amenities like financials, relationships and the negatively affected due to addiction. The addict is well aware, they've been stewing in guilt and shame of all these ramifications for years, so reminding or shaming will only destroy and due to the sensitivity of the addict, it could set them off. I feel the same way towards my parents now as in, they know, they have 2 decades of wisdom and knowledge of life ahead of me. That's why I don't understand why children think their parents don't know anything. I think, when a human realizes the best thing they can do, truly, is to appreciate and respect, value above all, the words and guidance of their parents and actually consume and follow whatever their advice is, then the human finally "gets it."

A huge step of maturity in the human experience has transpired. But when I say consume, I mean let this fill you up. Not just think or say. I relate this to the feeling you as a human get when you start to cry, it begins from the stomach, I believe, it's the purest human emotion. It's the most powerful emotion, so emotional, our body physically responds by perspiring a liquid substance from our irises. When you really think about it, the whole idea of crying is remarkable. The emotional symptoms include empathy, compassion, depression, pity, tolerance, understanding, realization, sorrow, purity and selflessness. It's beautiful. I haven't felt it for 7 years, drugs numb all emotions and almost make it impossible to shed tears.

Fentanyl after all, is designed for healthcare, loss of limbs, it's an ultimate pain relief. Addicts made it smokable, intoxicating. Numbing all emotions. My body never got a release. Just shows how powerful this drug is. It's taken jail, 6 months of methadone starting from 200ml, declining to 0. I've had to go through withdrawal hell from street drugs in January, and now as of today, May, my last dose of methadone forever. It's a bone eating and killing drug. Some argue it's worse than street drugs. It's basically like either having HIV or HERPES. It's not helping the addict at all, to me, it appears like a ploy for the government getting their piece of the cake in the drug world. They don't make money if people are healthy. It's a billion dollar industry. If they were trying to actually address and help the drug problem, jail interventions would and should be set up very differently to enforce sobriety, healing and recovery, not to give a liquid form of drug.

Little does anyone know, methadone is its own demon. Not only did I have to withdrawal from street drugs, they replaced it with methadone, and then I had to withdrawal from this as well coming out of jail. I go to court in the morning.

I noticed that Tyler had a glazed look over his face, we have the same drug of choice apparently. We layed in each of our beds with our eyes open, unable to sleep. I wonder if he will seek recovery and sobriety like I have. The sun started shining through our window which meant the guard would be coming to get me early for court at 7am. I guess I was feeling epic which is why I shared my story with this stranger, I got nothing to lose. It did feel good watching his facial expressions as I told my story, sometimes I forget how wild and intense it is/was, I am just so used to it.

I have been living with all this inside me with no one to tell, no one to share it with. My whole world is going to change today. I keep thinking, I would be lying if I said I wasn't anxious. Going to court in the past never ended well for me, especially on my sentencing days. I do feel like this time will be different because I feel like I have done the work, what will be, will be and that gives me a sense of patience and tolerance.

The universe already has a plan for me, so I am just going to have faith and let it play out how it is supposed to be. I knew it was morning. I could hear the keys approaching, my heart started to race and I thought to myself, this is it. I stood up and got my ugly white jail shoes on and said my goodbyes to Tyler and he wished me good luck. The guard stood at the door, "it's time for court".

I forgot that because it's sentencing, I have to appear in person back in Vancouver and the ride there is terribly uncomfortable but it will be the last time…hopefully. They make you get up at the crack of dawn, shackle you up, stick you in a rock hard bench in the back of a big moving truck in little metal cells, it's a bumpy ride. Then I get to city cells, unfortunately the officers there are horrible. The worst. They put me in a tiny cell from 9am-5:30pm. I had court at 2pm and luckily my new lawyer was tremendous at her job

She came in person to see me and discuss my court hearing beforehand, for the first time I actually knew what was going to happen before I entered the courtroom. I felt incredible, I was truly being rewarded for all my hard work in jail, turning my life around.

The Crown agreed to a joint submission which means I was getting released. For the first time I addressed the Crown, on record, with my mother present…before this I never had the courage to do so but my lawyer told me that if I were to petition I am a changed man, I should explain why and how. I was pacing back and forth in the waiting cell rehearsing my statement, I was confident until I actually was sitting in the courtroom and the judge was looking me in the eyes. I could feel my heart deflating but no matter what I wanted it on the court record that I had changed. I stood up when it was time to address the court and said:

"Someone could describe the birth of an airplane's climb into the upper atmosphere as bumpy, choppy, terrifying and full of turmoil, much like the last 7 years during my addiction. But really what is taking place is the miracle of flight. I reference this to the words used today about me and my unfortunate journey for the past several years, of course the words used to illustrate me are negative but what really has been taking place is a man battling the disease of addiction who is uneducated in the subject and has been dehumanized, unaware of how to heal my mental and emotional wounds, but by miracle, birthed recovery and sobriety.

First and foremost, I want to apologize to the court for not utilizing the very important time allotted for me constructively, my absence is unacceptable. As I reflect on my actions and crimes, along with the people that were a victim of my disease, I feel shameful, terrible and crippled with guilt and regret.

I've chosen to decline a high dose of methadone to none, on my own accord with the implication of not desiring any and all opioids, so I can operate my life at an optimum level. I have important family members that support me. I'm very blessed to have an intoxicatingly, unconditional, loving relationship with my mother Anne. She's unfailingly kind, extremely supportive and always remained my North Star in the darkness. She's my guidepost for everything. She makes it incredibly easy to respect her. She's my best friend, never giving up on me, even when I've given up on myself. My mother is unapologetically compassionate and empathetic, she never judges me even though I've given her reason to.

She houses my two little brothers Jeffrey and Jackson, both of which I share an unbreakable brotherly bond and hold with the utmost appreciation, love and devotion. As well, my older sister Jaymie whom I share my childhood with. She is supremely bright, academically gifted and specializes in healing and spiritual work and is supporting my recovery as we correspond my past trauma with her teachings. She shows me tolerance and patience. Living among these special individuals will set myself up for success as I return into the community. I have a community transition team leader to help me embrace my new reality with recovery. My dad Lee and step mom Sarah, other younger brother Connor and younger sister Katie also help supplement my success in sobriety and recovery, they are my twin pillars, without which I could not stand.

I've used this time to hyperdrive my sobriety, I'm changing my life. I'm employed on the unit, a member of AA and NA, practiced religion with my peers and chaplain, completed classes to sharpen my scholastic side, and participated in arts and crafts. I chose to do positive things with my time. I now understand why professionals correlate drug addiction with being sick and diseased. I had traumatic things happen to me when I moved to Vancouver.

I was introduced to using destructive methods to mend my suffering. It destroyed me, my heart broke several times and so many devastating incidents. My life became completely unmanageable and I became something and someone I didn't know. I'm comforted with the fact that my mistakes don't define me and now I've learnt, and am still learning how to mend my scars constructively.

I'm stronger and wiser now in my sobriety now, turning around my downward spiral. In some cases I may have acted alone, some I was influenced and baited by others, however I realize it doesn't matter as I am fully responsible for my own behavior. During the chaos, in losing myself, I forgot what a hardworking, loving, charismatic person I am. I want to beat the disease of addiction and I've established a deep relationship with my high power. I let myself down and my family down but I refuse to let any of this be my demise.

As per my AA/NA work, I've written my entire family a 32 page amends letter seeking their forgiveness and understanding full of my rigorously honest explanation of my absence.

I can't change the past but I can regain control of my future. I know I'm capable of incredible things and I'm eagerly, looking forward to proving I'm a changed man. I plan on showing my integrity properly and positively to my family and to my community, as I've been raised to do. Hope and faith entered my life again. I am taking my life back."

My time in court was a pivotal moment in my life, and the new direction I would be taking. What would happen in this courtroom, could change the course of my entire life. After I spoke, the judge asked me to turn to my mom and apologize for what I put her through so I turned ,with tears in my eyes and said, "I'm sorry, I love you". She was sobbing as I left the courtroom a free man. I felt the weight on my shoulders evaporate.

I felt like the judge and the Crown saw the conviction in my words and the desire to change in my body language, I was serious about altering the direction in my life and I couldn't help but feel proud that because I truly did the work, I was being rewarded from my higher power. It allowed me to understand why I was put back in jail each time, because I remained unchanged and unmoved. After court, I was put back in a cell and waited hours for my paperwork to go through. Although the wait was long the feeling of ecstasy as I walked out of the jail doors as a free man was worth the wait. It was so powerful. All consuming. The clothes they gave me to wear were simple, handed to me as I signed my release papers, but they felt like a second skin- stiff, unfamiliar. I had dreamed of this moment, imagined it countless times in my cell. But now that it was real, the fear was as strong as the hope. The road ahead was full of unknowns, and the familiar ache of old habits whispered at the back of my mind.

As I walked away from the courthouse in Vancouver, I clutched the small clear plastic garbage bag that held the few belongings I had managed to accumulate. It wasn't much. A couple books, letters from family, a worn out journal, but they were the pieces of my past that I was determined to carry with me into my new life, reminders of where I had been and where I needed to go. My mom was around the corner waiting for me in her truck for the trip back home to Langley and away from Vancouver. Another display of support, I thank God for giving me a mother like her in this life. I can honestly say, if it wasn't for her, I wouldn't be here. Even though I shielded her from a lot of what I was going through, I tried to call her all throughout the years whenever I could and she handled me with grace, each time with a smile, trying to be supportive and positive, even when I called her in tears, which was often. She never missed a call. Giving up on me wasn't an option for her. I can only imagine what it would be like to have to watch your child, best friend, battle addiction, and she told me that everytime the phone rang over the years, she was just waiting to get that call, the call that her son was dead, but here I was finally in front of her, not only a free man from crime, but a free man from the disease of addiction. All of this horror, all of these

chapters, were finally closed. I could now begin a new chapter, the very best is yet to come.

I was finally home, I got out of the truck and walked up the front steps to the house, my hand hesitated on the doorknob. This was it- the moment I have somehow feared. I wasn't sure what to expect on the other side. I wasn't even sure who I was anymore. But I knew if I didn't open that door, I'd never find out. The door swung open before I could decide, and there stood my two "little" brothers, eyes brimming with tears. They looked older than I remembered, the lines on their face deeper and their hair streaked with change. But their smiles were the same, full of love and relief. They welcomed me home, pulling me in for a big hug. Their arms were bulky and the strength of their embrace was undeniable. I hadn't seen them in what felt like a lifetime. The familiar smell of the house washed over me- cooking, old wood, the faint smell of lavender. It was like stepping back in time, and yet, everything was different. I was different. The house was warm, inviting, but I couldn't shake the feeling that I didn't quite belong here anymore. Not yet. I was free, but freedom is terrifying. I hadn't walked these halls as a free man in years, and the world had changed while I was locked away and lost in addiction. More importantly, I had changed. I was a shell of my former self. Bigger, gaunt, with dark circles under my eyes and a tremor in my hands. It was extremely euphoric to see my brothers, and sisters. I felt very estranged, out of place, a different kind of lost. Everyone was very supportive of me, but internally, my anxiety was aggressive. I couldn't sleep for the first week, my mom and I shared her comfy king size bed together , she wanted me to be in her space and just enjoy the time we now have together. To make up for lost time. My recovery was far from easy, it was a daily battle, a struggle to rebuild my life from the ground up. Getting my ID's renewed, bank accounts revived, new room and clothes back in place.

I attended group meetings and worked through the steps again, one by one. There were moments of doubt, and times when the urge to give up was overwhelming. But I kept going, driven by the memory of the darkness I had faced in prison and all the detox and withdrawal. My family's thoughts and feelings during my addiction were all very different. It's interesting having people I love have all of these harsh words towards me, the addict, and the fact that they thought that I was in too deep and wouldn't make it out alive, but here I am. I was there, in front of each of them, looking them in the eyes, beating all odds.

Sometimes I do forget how miraculous it is that I am now living happily sober. It was like it finally clicked for me, and I just unzipped the traumatized addict costume and stepped out of it because I was finally ready to wear the strong emotionally healthy and sober costume. It finally fit.

The one thing I am really honored about is the fact that I had a closing statement in the court, now everything I said is on the court record. I was extremely nervous, and as I said, in the past I didn't have the courage to speak on my own behalf and I thank sobriety, it gave me the clarity in my mind to be able to formulate and have the ability to put my thoughts into words. I felt like because I actually meant what I said about changing my life, it's almost like they knew and somehow did their research before deciding whether or not they would release me.

It was amazing to be back where I belonged, around the people I am supposed to be with. They say that the time you enter addiction is the place you get stuck in even after it's over. I was 25 when I began my days of addiction and at that time my family's home was very different. My two younger brothers were little and now they are grown men with lovely girlfriends.

The days after my return were a blur of adjustments. Simple things, like making my bed or choosing what to eat for breakfast, felt overwhelming. The structure of prison life had been suffocating, but it had also been a crutch. Out here, the choices are mine again, and that made me feel uneasy. I had been my own worst enemy before, and I didn't trust myself not to fall back into old patterns. But I had made a promise to myself in those quiet, solitary nights. I had worked hard in the recovery programs, pouring over every word in the 12-step guide, wrestling with my demons. I knew that if I didn't keep moving forward, I'd be swallowed by the past. I spent hours in my old room which now felt like a strangers' place. I reread the letters I had received during my sentence, trying to reconnect with the people I had hurt, the life I had lost. My parents are supportive, patient, but I can see the worry in their eyes, the fear that I might slip, that I might undo all the work I have done. It was a fear we shared.

Everything looked different and all the routines of everyone's days were very overwhelming for me. I did feel very estranged, I didn't like feeling like a stranger to my family's home. Everything felt very uncomfortable. I had work to do. I came home with an open heart and mind, humbly with grace and tolerance. My mission was to win back their trust, rebuild my relationship with my whole family, to get our unshakable bond back in place. My room was changed a bit, so I went out and bought myself a new 55" RCA flatscreen TV to watch my shows. I am someone that spends a lot of time in their room. I set up my new computer to continue my writing, as well as organizing my clothes that I received from different family members and friends. I also bought a new air conditioner for my room. I can't sleep without noise and I like a cold environment while I sleep. Each night when I lay down in my bed my mind would race. I needed to be patient.

The days turned into weeks, and slowly, a routine began to form. I want anyone that I hurt to feel validated, however they may feel towards me. I am well aware of all the damage I caused them all. I keep in mind that as hard as my life was and all the stuff I went through, it's not a "pissing" competition between my hell and theirs. Mine is not greater than theirs.

At home there was some hesitation when they found out I would be there all day, alone, while they were at work, leaving all their expensive things alone in the house ,with me. That would never have happened if I was in an active addiction and I don't blame them, it's been humbling earning my stripes back with each of them. On the first morning ,when my mom had to go to work and my brothers were gone as well to their jobs, I had a night terror and woke up crying. I still have vicious visualizations of my past events because each of them was quite traumatizing.

I went and laid in my mothers bed with her and had tears running down my face. This was the first time in my sobriety that I felt like I wanted my mommy. I realized that I wanted my words to carry weight, so I have also made it my mission to be a man of my word. When I say I am going to do something then I will do it. If I say I am going to be somewhere then I will be there.

The relationship with my family grew stronger each week. We all openly talked about the past, about the pain we had all endured. There were tears, but there was also healing. I know I have a long way to go, that trust would take time to rebuild, but we all were on that path together. And so, I kept moving forward, I was court ordered to see my community transition team leader and peer worker every monday. As well as my probation officer, whenever he deemed it necessary. In my meetings with my peer worker there was a real connection and I looked up to him. I wanted to be there and do what he was doing through his lived addiction story. I asked about how he got to where he was now, and he told me the schooling and certifications I needed to take. I decided to pursue this and I did. It gave me something to focus on, other than writing my book.

My support team was incredibly proud of my discipline especially when they found out that I had completed my schooling and was now a fully certified Peer Support Worker and able to work for BC Mental Health and Addictions Society.

The success rate for recovered addicts is very low and even lower for the ones that actually stay sober. I humbly know that I am a rare breed and my resilience shines down any negative doubts that people may have of me, or even maybe some that I still share for myself. I have been asked by many people what my secret is or how am I doing it? How am I successful in this miraculous recovery because so many people are struggling with addiction. It would be selfish of me not to try and help.

I made sure that I had my village set up, even the strongest characters need help and it's okay to need help. I have cousins that are in sobriety and recovery, I talk to them very often, as well as my immediate family. I know I can talk to my family about anything, but I needed to make sure that I put up my new boundaries for myself and others. I need to understand the kind of people I want in my life and the kind of people I don't. When I make new friends, I look for different qualities now when deciding if that friendship is a healthy choice. One of the keys to watch out for is jealousy. The people that make comments like "oh that would be nice to afford that" or "I wish I could look like that", these are selfish people's responses. I look for people that congratulate me or are happy that I am happy. I am very weary of who I allow in my circle. I know what happens when I let negative people around me. I know what I offer in friendship and I now expect the same in return. No more excuses for other peoples misgivings or unacceptable behavior.

I have tons of aspirations for careers, a few of them involve a criminal record check. My record was a barrier, one that I had expected but still find disheartening. I never worried about those three words until now, as my new reality, as positive as I am at making everything work, I can't run away from the past. Unfortunately all of my choices have consequences whether I was set up or not. I understand the saying that "I made my bed and now I have to lay in it. "

The way I handled disappointing news in the past was I would fly off the handle and try to escape. My emotional maturity truly is showing here. It's amazing now that I have new tools like tolerance, patience and grace, along with humility, I now look at roadblocks as a sudden universal change in direction instead of a dead end stop.

One major issue that has been difficult to deal with is what has happened with Jason. Before, while I was writing from within the bars of jail, we couldn't communicate because we kept missing the strategic times, so I never knew where his mind was at and it left me to wonder and assume the worst possible reasons as to why he didn't make an effort to talk and connect. It turned out that he was trying to send me letters. He then figured out because we are co-accused, that the jail would intercept all of his attempts to talk to me. He sent the letters that he wrote to me to his mom in Ontario and she then tried to send them back to me.

I never received them, for some reason the records department wouldn't allow me to. I have been able to talk to his mom about the whole situation, now that I am out. But in my 18 months probation contract I am still not to talk to him or anyone that has any affiliation with him from our past life. If I am to breach, I would have to do the remaining months back in jail, behind bars. Not happening!

I promised my family that I will take all the conditions seriously, and if my probation officer were to ask them any questions, which he said he would, I will not put them in a position to lie.. My word means everything to me now, and I want them to hold value while I am sober. Jason started to call me in the first few weeks here and there, while I have been at home here in Langley. I had a deep conversation with my family and decided that as hard as it is because there are feelings there between me and Jason, it can't happen right now.

I asked my probation officer how I would go about getting the part of my probation regarding Jason taken out but nothing can happen right now only after he is released, potentially a few more weeks. The court can't communicate with him while he is in jail. It does bother me that for some reason he doesn't have it on his conditions that he can't talk to me, only I have the condition that I can't talk to him which I will follow. But Jason still tried to meet with me even though he knew I would be risking my freedom in doing so. It bothers me that he isn't looking out for my well being. If it were reversed, I wouldn't ever risk putting him in jail on my account. I would support him in following his conditions and not try to violate them. If he truly does love me, why would he risk taking my freedom away and by extension, if I were to get caught, to take me away from him? Why would he want that?

I had a hard conversation with his mom and told her that I have to sever all ties right now, it was imperative to follow the law especially right now. During our conversation she said to me, that if he didn't have me she thought that he would relapse and be back on the streets in Vancouver where we left off. I admitted to her that saying that to me wasn't fair, to put any pressure on me. Being educated in recovery and sobriety now I realize that when things like that are said to me all I can think of is the individual saying it or doing it has lots of work to do, because in order to recover, blame simply isn't an element.

He has to be able to stand on his own two feet, happy and sober before even thinking about being in a relationship. His mother did later apologize for what she said and clarified what she really meant to say, so I forgave her. I never did take it on anyway. My recovery has given me ironclad armor that protects me from statements like that and I see what the person really means when they speak.

I get asked all the time, while I'm in recovery, if I miss using drugs. I think that we all do think about it, thoughts come and go. I would be lying if I said I haven't thought about it but my reasons seem to have changed. I am over the past, everything I did and the crimes I committed I feel like in the eyes of the law because of my jail time and standing in court, my debt is paid off.

Now I feel like I am facing other reasons for wanting to use, I think sometimes I feel like well can I not use it to have fun? Can I control it? If I am not using it as an escape then is that any different? I argue with myself all the time, the proper Jeremy is giving me that look of "are you fucking kidding me, doing crystal meth or fentanyl is not an acceptable hobby, you idiot!"

Not exactly an activity that I would want my future husband to participate in so I would imagine whoever marries me, most likely, wouldn't want their husband doing drugs as a pastime. As well, it's all downhill from there, I know this and then I start to focus on the root of the actual desire of wanting to use… why do I want to?

When I start to cross examine myself I realize that it is because I am bored, I am still on probation and I have to be home by 9pm and can't leave anywhere till 6am which makes it very difficult to get a job. A lot of places don't hire when someone doesn't have an open availability and court conditions. My job right now is to stay sober and follow my conditions, that is my job and if I am doing that then I am doing okay.

It would appear that the times that I seek to use or want drugs is when something inside of me is not feeling right. When I reflect back to before, when using drugs wasn't yet an option, I remember feeling strong emotions which is why I struggled with depression. When things didn't go my way or I realized I have this huge void in my life, I would try to fill the void with men or women...or things.

I think this was because before I didn't have a relationship with my higher power. I am finding the high in honesty, and being a man of my word. This situation with Jason is difficult now, he is in jail but is being released in six days. We still have the condition that we aren't allowed to talk to each other until my probation is over. He has called me several times and when I tell my mother she gets super angry. I understand her anger. She thinks I am going to fall into the same trap because when he gets released, she believes my heart will get drawn back towards him.

I had a meeting with my probation officer, I was honest with him and told him that Jason contacted me and was released to a recovery house. Ken handled it really well. I felt good, he could have breached me but he understood and because I am following all the very important conditions he let this one slide. Now if my mom were to contact Ken and ask if I told him about contact from Jason, he can say yes Jeremy did tell me and if Ken were to ask my mom the same question she would agree.. So now I do not have to put anyone in the position of lying for me.

Maybe I am overcompensating because during my addiction my words meant nothing, so now that I am not in addiction, they mean everything. After all the people I have been in love with I realize the one person that I should love more is myself. That little voice in my head that told me every time I got cheated on that I deserved better, I didn't listen to it, even though it was always with me, it never betrayed me but I betrayed it. That little voice that said I shouldn't be here, even though I found myself in places I shouldn't have been. That's the self love I speak of that I need to rebuild, relove. Refine. I of all people understand that damaged people have the real capacity to damage people, places or things. That is why the relationship I rebuild with myself is key, to heal all the damage that has been inflicted on me either by me or others. Doesn't really matter how or who, only what the end result is…healing. No one is born evil or corrupt. No one is born an addict or born with trauma.

Trauma defined is a deeply distressing or disturbing experience: "a personal trauma like the death of a child". The synonyms are injury, damage, hurt, wound, wounding, sore, bruise, cut, laceration, lesion, abrasion, contusion. The antonyms are: healing. There is no wound too deep, no bruise to black and blue or no heart so broken that it can't succumb to be healed.

We as humans are resilient. For so many years whenever I depended on anyone, during my addiction, my trust was shattered, my very own heart suffered from laceration and many abrasions with too many contusions to count. My soul is damaged and my spirit is so sore. Many of the damaged people that I surrounded myself with thought that I was a lost cause and that I would die a junkie on the streets.

Before getting back home here, when I looked in the mirror, the person looking back at me was a soulless stranger with dark jaded eyes and a hurting corrupt mind barely able to grasp a positive thought. I learned as I navigated the shark infested waters of addiction that I would either sink or swim, and even if I could swim it wasn't long until a shark came along and bit my head off. I needed a dolphin. I needed a hero. A hero comes in all shapes and sizes. As hard as it is to open myself up and face the music, it was the only way that I could finally find my lost friend called healing. I became my own hero.

Staying sober is one thing but that's not all recovery consists of. Recovery requires healing, sobriety is lady peace giving the opportunity to use the tools needed to embrace recovery and to embrace the main component which is the ability to heal all wounds…all traumas. To shatter through PTSD.

As an addict I look at myself as an onion with many layers. The outside layer is drugs and the use of drugs as a cover. Once I was able to successfully peel that off I can relate this idea to sobriety. Now the onion can actually be cut up and diced and each layer of trauma can be analyzed.

Being an addict and using drugs is the byproduct of a traumatized human. The harder they use, the more traumatized they are. My higher power assisted me in admitting that I was powerless and no human power could restore me which allowed me to finally meet God.

There's a reason why me, an addict, choose to believe in God…it's because I have met the devil. He has been breathing down my neck and ruthlessly keeps chasing away the angels desperately trying to break through to me and protect me, but the devil's will is usually unmatched. Darkness swallowed all the light that I once had, when I first arrived in Vancouver.

There was a death that night when I left Langley to Vancouver.. The death of an innocent kid whose light shined pure and whose soul still remained genuine and untouched. In the blazing inferno of despair and flames of trauma that innocent kid, like I once was, turned to ashes. Thanks to sobriety and recovery, from within the ashes, a blinding light managed to penetrate through the darkness. The ashes consisted of a characterized toxic tragedy of unhappiness and an unpleasantness with a starless gloom.

Deep within this shadow birthed a sparkling and intensely dazzling incandescent luminescent phoenix. In its brilliance it radiates intense hope and gleaming faith finally aglow. I now begin to rise shiny and newly polished. A reborn man ablaze with phosphorescent mental health, it twinkles a lustrous shimmering me. After I was erected I still needed human companionship and help. In the steps of recovery many of the steps are self determination based, but some of the most important ones require another to assist.

In the past whenever I opened up to anyone and showed vulnerability it was targeted methodically and used to attack me in the newly founded weak point. I had to trust in the process and in my higher power to hold my hand while I let myself trust one more time. The most important time, trusting in the divine. I lost my life that night in the inferno. I have been seeking it ever since, battling the hands of time and the twists and turns of fate while carefully crafting the demise of each layer I covered myself with during my catastrophic war with addiction.

I spend a lot of time wondering about my house, thinking and pondering about my new reality at home. A spiritual awakening is exactly what it sounds like. My spirit has been awakened after a long dark sleep…I probably was roofied, but I am very much alive now, my spirit is fiercely awake after a dreadful slumber. In the past days when I let addiction creep into my thoughts, I used to worry, but that worry is starting to subside.

Some people say that's the addict mind kicking in, something that I will be stuck with for the rest of my life because I am an addict. However, I don't agree with that. When I do have moments of weakness or perhaps miss certain aspects of my previous life in Vancouver I do something very clever. I play the tape. I play it out in my mind how my relapse would appear. It would ruin my family's trust and respect for me. It would destroy my mother's love for me, she will never hate me, but instead she would be wickedly disappointed.

One of the most common questions I am asked is "what was my epiphany moment when I realized I didn't want to be a junkie anymore?" Although there are many little things that made me realize I needed a change as you now know. Yet one of the more prominent moments occurred after I had my third seizure and I was hospitalized in jail. I was put into a room with another woman who was in her sixties, she was laying in the hospital bed beside me and every morning her forty year old son would come to sit with her for breakfast and support. I thought about myself and if my mom was ever hospitalized that I wouldn't even be able to make a phone call, I would miss out on being there for her and that thought shook me.

When I was arrested this January, I had been talking ,the day before, with my mom on the phone. I was high in my SRO downtown Vancouver on Powell Street bawling and severely depressed and all I could think was I can't get any higher. There isn't any other drug I can do so the strongest one still isn't working, I'm still hating my life, something needs to change. I have come so far, I have followed all my conditions and have a great relationship with my probation officer.

My ambitions run wild, I hope one day they make a movie out of my book because I want to inspire and help as many people as I can. Everytime I found myself shocked in whatever new crazy scenario I was in, I always thought that the world needed to know about this. I must bring awareness. Not only with addiction but in helping other people who move to a random city and fall in love with all the wrong people and then use your heart to undo all you are. The people that prey on uneducated ,innocent minds and hearts and install drugs and crime into your life to better theirs. To raise awareness to all the evil out there and be a cautionary tale of life and death, luckily I still have my life even though many tried to take it away and even tried to make me believe that I didn't deserve life or want it anymore.

As I said before, I don't like the idea of being called an addict for the rest of my life. I choose not to believe that is what defines me. If I dissect that statement it would really mean that I have turned to drugs in times of peril and due to the mental state I was in at the time. I allowed myself to use drugs. I used destructive means instead of constructive. So someone who has murdered another human in a time of peril and wasn't in the proper state of mind or good mental status, can't be cured? Once a murderer always a murderer? Once an addict always an addict? I think no matter what the topic is, it's circumstantial, I can't change what I turned to in the past but with revolutionary educational awareness I can change what I choose to turn to in times of trouble now and in the future. Thus, I will not be an "addict" for the rest of my life if I choose not to be. I have the power, not the drugs. It isn't that I will be an addict for the rest of my life, it's that wiring that has been engraved in my mind that I will have to work on and not default to old habits. That will be my issue. I just have to lead with grace and patience, and I do truly believe that what will happen, and what is meant to be, will be. I crawled from the depths of hell, some would say I was in the deepest of depths in addiction, a place where not many creep out of alive and here I am.

Now that I have rigorously house cleaned my mentality and morality, dealt with my demons and now I am aware of my defects and fears while resolving my past traumas, there is no longer a need for an outer layer of protection. I now possess the tools to be able to handle any disappointment that may come my way and deal with it with grace and tolerance. I hope to lead with a life of faith and hope, with the desire for good and walking with my higher power.

It makes the unknown and uncertainty exciting because there are so many different ways my life may go and I truly believe that God will take me in the direction that I am meant to travel so I won't have anxiety any more. I get to choose what I am and what I am not. I will not let addiction, the cold hard bitch, determine who and what I am, as it did in the past. I am no longer weak, the addiction won't be able to control me anymore. My standards are back in place and there's no room at my table anymore for addiction. She can't sit with me anymore and I say that with my head up high.

Staying sober is a job on its own and I beat myself up because I have so much free time and I don't give myself enough credit for how much of a job it is on its own to stay sober all day. As long as I am breathing soberly, I am doing my job just fine. More than fine. Plus the plans I have for the newly found me, are tremendous. The transition time right now for me, with all this peace and quiet, is uncomfortable. I have been catching up on a lot of shows that I missed during my addiction and I have been rebuilding important friendships that I let sink for the past 7 years.

I am enjoying certain perks of sobriety, for me being able to be contacted through a working cell phone and phone number so that my people can contact me in times of trouble and need, like my little brother Connor. Having him cry on the phone tells me what is going on in his life - needing my help and support and being able to give it. All these mend major cuts on my soul. Having him say, "brother you have no idea how much it means to me to be able to finally have you back and be able to call you for help, I love you so much." It means the world to me and if I was high downtown Vancouver none of this could happen. I got to be a part of my little sister's graduation. I was able to see my older sister off as she moved her life to Alberta. I am able to see my grandma every Monday evening for dinner. I even have time to finally spend time with my dad and go dirt biking. I've been present for a few of my family member's birthdays since being home and sober. It's rewarding.

If I can do it then anyone can do it. It is not easy and it takes a lot of courage and strength to successfully find my lost life, but it is obtainable. Once I realized I was worth more than I was selling myself for and the standard I allowed myself to live by, that's when my wings grew back and I was able to once again fly. Now I can fly higher and longer, faster and stronger and I would never be able to be where I am now if it weren't for all the horror I had lived through.

It is never too late to make a change. If I want to seek it can be sought. Addiction is cunning and destroys many incredible human beings, it's taken a lot of great lives away from this world as many couldn't reach sobriety and recovery, perhaps moving forward with writing this book I will be able to help other talented colorful individuals find their lost life before it's too late.

So many people and so many families are searching for a miraculous cure to help their addict in need, or maybe for themselves, I feel. People wonder what magical clinical therapy or treatment facility works and will save the issue of addiction. Truth is, the best thing an addict can use is a peer support worker or someone that helps support and inspire self determination.

There is no cure, the only thing that saved me, was me. I learned from other people's stories of their own addiction and what they went through and how they coped and applied it to my own life. When I felt validated and found someone, something that made me feel relatable, found someone that shared mutual addiction and mental health struggles, that made all the difference.

The first step was getting sober so that my mind could be in a place to start to properly function and see things with clarity. Then came the emotional work with my traumas, I used the steps in AA and NA to help me as well as some help from bible studies. I used my support systems like my community transition team leader and my very own peer worker that made me see that it is possible, I can do it. It gave me hope and something to work towards. Once I could see that it was possible, I knew I had a chance, if I wanted it. I think that I am not the only one, that during my addiction that a little voice inside my head kept telling me that I was better than a life during addiction and I deserve better.

Anytime I had horrible things happen to me I could feel the angels in my aura standing tall on one of my shoulders, equally appalled. Drugs truly make everything worse, but they are the easiest solution, especially when I felt alone and lost, when I had easy access to them or had used them in the past for fun.

Using them for fun can easily turn into something not fun and they took over my power. The mind is a powerful thing and when I truly wanted a change it was there for me ready to start thinking differently.

Many would think that there's no possible way I could ever love and trust again. Losing in love is better than never loving at all, I am a firm believer in that. I realized it's not about not loving again, it is about protecting my heart and not letting love control it anymore. I now have boundaries and my mind is closely tied together with my heart instead of letting my heart make the decisions.

I am wiser now in knowing that people have the capacity to hurt, and to deceive. I am now taking in everything I have learned so that when I meet my next great love, I will only give my heart to the one that knows how to treat it properly and nothing less than perfection will be acceptable. Love is supposed to be beautiful and unconditional, it is supposed to be a benefit adding another person into my life especially when giving my heart and if it's a negative thing then it doesn't have a place in my life moving forward. I've already had new deceptions try to corrupt my joy. I had someone contact me and my mother regarding the book I am writing, trying to get information about it, trying to stop me from getting it published. They impersonated a top newspaper company to steal details and try to discourage me from proceeding. I had forgotten the lengths that some people will go to, to try and ruin something great. I think the best idea is to keep the people from my past, in my past.

I haven't gone through hell and back to be treated like shit again or be deceived. I don't care moving forward about someone else's baggage and I am not making excuses for someone else anymore. When I meet the next lover I am not going to treat them less than they deserve because of my past. If anything I am going to treat them better because I don't want them to ever feel how I have felt in the past.

Everyone has a reason to be a bitch, it doesn't mean they have a right to be. I can either grow and learn from my past or I can let it deplete me and render me useless and unchanged. As far as addiction goes, the only thing that someone can do to help an addict is let them know that you are there for them and you won't let them go or ever leave them. That doesn't mean give them money or alter your life to help change or correct theirs because it doesn't matter if you have millions and are the most powerful person in the world, there is nothing you can do for an addict if they aren't ready for change. As long as they are in addiction there is nothing that can be done, all you can do is support them in letting them know they won't ever be alone and you are there for them whenever they are ready and willing to make changes.

No one could save me…I am finding that the days that I have been tempted to use and it is prominent in my mind, when I reach out to support it makes it better. I tell my mother or my cousins that are also in AA and NA, practicing recovery, and I am brutally honest with them. At first I hesitated in doing this because I was scared that they would judge or perhaps I just didn't want to worry them and have them think that my sobriety or recovery is in danger, but the reactions I am getting are far from them being worried.

They have all seemed relieved that I am being open and honest with them about my struggles, it makes them think that I am not hiding and skulking around their backs conspiring of ways to use or how I could use and get away with it, even imagine how my relapse would look. Honestly, truth is the best policy with a recovering addict. I reflect on all the things I am able to do due to me being sober on a day to day basis. Instead of being in a state of hopelessness, this is something, as you now know, that I experienced and lived with for years.

The first step to fixing my problem was to acknowledge there is one. The worst thing that I could do was to tell myself that I couldn't do it or I would casually always say in my mind and out loud that there's no way I will ever be sober again. It was toxic. I changed the narrative and I would recommend everyone do the same because I am living proof that anyone can do it just like I did and believe me when I say, it's never too late to recover and no wound so great that it can't be healed. I want to be a beacon of hope and inspiration for other addicts that are battling trauma and addiction. I want to be a cautionary tale, or if I can prevent someone from going through what I went through, I would consider my duty fulfilled. This shit is real. There is real horror out there in the world, I want to warn people that are diving into the dark side of the world like I did, to be very careful especially those that are experimenting in the sex trade. The success and the high of being desired, wanted, is ecstasy…but it's playing with fire. If you don't have your wits about you, you'll get burned. The people that were in my life during that period, they all wanted something from me, they weren't around me for good and healthy reasons. It was hard to pick the bad from the good.

In my new reality I am finding staying sober is one thing, but working recovery is another battle in itself. As I sit in my room I realize I can obtain sobriety, but that doesn't mean I am recovering. I get asked a lot how I am doing it, how does someone stay sober and not relapse. I believe it will be my duty to assist with the drug crisis in this world. So many recovered addicts don't have the mental and emotional capacity, as well as still being mentally scholastically sharp, to be able to hold a high position in society. I feel that I do. I have proper compassion and empathy for the drug addict as well as understanding how they are affecting innocent people in the community.

They shouldn't suffer the consequences of someone else's addiction disease. I think I can be the buffer, I can assist in the solution, I can be that bridge.

That means I will be working on my recovery everyday. Jason will be released back into the community after his court ordered recovery house stunt is complete, which is only 4 weeks long. He can still stay there or go back to Vancouver. I was devastated because there is nothing I can say to persuade him into doing the right thing. I finally understand now how everyone I loved felt every time I was incarcerated and chose to return to Vancouver to relapse and continue using drugs. No matter how much they loved me, I wasn't ready. I felt the same thing with Jason.

Jason said it has clicked for him just as it did for me. I am proud of him and perhaps our love story isn't at its end. However, he may be sober but I am finding that his behavior is still the same as when he was on drugs. I realize that we don't even know each other as sober men and that we would have to reintroduce each other to the new versions of ourselves. My mind is different and my body is different, maybe we won't even be attracted to one another. When he called me from his recovery house, I felt like he was just sweeping our past under the rug and for me to even think of moving forward with him. I felt that we needed to discuss all the things that he did to me.

We discussed the times that he came towards me with rage in his eye, the time he destroyed my studio apartment and scared me. So many times I had to defend myself from his violence, so many times he let me down and wasn't there for me and never had my back. He always got caught in lies and cheated on me with other men. Now everything he says I simply just don't believe. I put it on him and asked him what he did when his ex cheated on him, did he ever trust him again? Was it ever the same after that took place and that trust was broken? He answered no. I then asked, so what would you have me do...? Silence.

Trust is the bond that makes any relationship work, once it's taken away it's hard to make things stay together without the bonding agent of trust.

My recovery and sobriety is paramount, me and Jason got into a fight today and after going back and forth he said that maybe he should take a step back from me because he doesn't want to jeopardize these two things and I quickly replied, no one and nothing will jeopardize it, only I have the power…not you. As we were arguing, I saw the old him trying his old tricks, trying to belittle me and make me feel stupid or wrong in how I was feeling. He wasn't supportive and I just didn't like the way he made me feel. I feel like I am above this shit now. I closed this chapter already. I am not the same weak little stupid easy manipulated boy that was high all the time and easy to fool. He tried talking down to me but realized I wasn't down there anymore…I am way above it now. This made me feel proud of myself. This behavior won't fly anymore. When I call him on his attitude or rudeness, he deflects. He thinks he's being smooth, but it couldn't be more rough.

He is realizing that how he was/is won't work with who I am now. He says he feels like he isn't good enough for me now and I respond by telling him that it's up to him in the way that he knows what my standards and requirements are and he can either step up or step out. This is the first real time I noticed true growth and having my own back, sticking up for myself, which I hadn't done in years. I am not letting myself down anymore or allowing people to treat me like shit. This doesn't mean I hate Jason, it just means he has to heal and fix himself . shows why no one should get into a relationship while working on recovery, at first, because the addict needs to focus on themself. We all deserve happiness, and I applaud him for his sobriety at the very least.

I can understand why my mother and my family are so hesitant with him because all they can remember is all the times that I called them crying when he did something to me in the past. I need to understand that this is why they don't want me to have anything to do with anyone in my past during addiction, because they all destroyed me. I need to respect them and I do understand where they are coming from. I would feel the same way if I were them and the situation was reversed. If one of my family members were in an abusive relationship and called me crying all the time telling me they were getting attacked, stolen from and constantly hurt by someone, I would want to "kill" that person and ask them to have nothing to do with them. The excuse of addiction only goes so far, and it doesn't take away from the abusive behavior that took place especially for the supportive family members standing by.

I really don't fight fate anymore and I don't worry so much about the future because I feel like what is going to happen will happen so there really isn't any sense stressing or worrying about it.

In my room I have my computer and the other day I looked at my old facebook posts from 2020 I realized that I said I was going to make a book about everything that has happened to me, I completely forgot about it and here I am making sure I complete my book. I spend a lot of my time during the day working on it. For some reason I have felt very compelled to make sure I successfully write and publish it for the whole world to read.

When I first got released and everyone celebrated my new sober life and getting me back I got all the attention. As time went on the novelty wore off but I now see why people in recovery say that it's smart to work your recovery everyday. It is, because no matter how much time passes by, the addict needs to always remember how important and how miraculous my sobriety is, to always cherish it and hold it close because it truly is a gift. A gift that many addicts spend their whole life trying to get. I need to never forget how magnificent it is that I wake up and I am sober, I breathe sober air and I am not a slave to a drug and I only have myself to thank. I am grateful for now being present and celebrating big family events like birthdays and graduations.

I can see how much my family loves that I am finally here and aware of the life going on all around me. These are the things I never thought I would ever witness again, more than half the time I didn't even know what day of the week it was.

It was all a blur. I missed my life every day and no matter what I did I never thought I would ever find it again. When I would think about how I could get it back it felt like it was this big monster that I couldn't ever find the courage and strength to tackle it. So many people from that dark world thought that I was a lost cause and the people that used and abused me would smirk at my stupidity and lack of knowledge thinking I would die a junkie with no redeeming qualities. They thought they had me beat and that I was too weak to ever find myself again, thinking they were successful in ruining me and my life, mocking me and laughing among one another... The feeling is euphoric now eradicating the damage they did and regaining my power, my life. Looks like I got the last laugh. I know this is my ego talking when I say that but I really can't help but feel this way.

The days have been passing by, I celebrated my six months sobriety today. I asked my sister Jaymie and younger brother Jeffrey to support me by going to an AA/NA meeting with me here in Langley. I was given a symbolic six month shiny new token as a congratulations. My family bought me an ice cream cake and sung me a song later in the night. It means a lot to me.

As I lay in my room inside my house, which I spend a lot of time doing these days, the contrast between being in a jail cell and here is colossal. It took me a minute to get my sense of style and normal human daily functions back in place. I feel free, finally, obviously, physically, but also mentally. There's life going on all around me which is really cool because in jail it was stagnant. My mom's house is really bougie, the cupboards are stacked with all sorts of foods, the bathrooms have an abundance of beauty products, it's mental.

Before jail I was on the streets so I had nothing, I haven't been in a house that's fully stocked in years. The decor is incredible, especially since the room I have been in for the last six months was simply barren and lifeless, cold. Finally I have technology back in my life, especially having a nice phone, and when I go to bed and wake up it is still there! I used to have to hide anything of value under my clothes or in areas of my body otherwise it would go missing.

I have a sense of peace and comfort, something that I haven't had in so long. Knowing that I am safe, my personal belongings are safe is something I took for granted before because when I lost that, it replaced it with fear and anxiety. Now I smell the fused incense I have in my room and all different sorts of perfumes and colognes that each of my family members wear including myself floating around in the house. My cute new air conditioner is purring, my big fancy new TV is playing my favorite shows. I feel like I can truly thrive here in my little bubble that I have created and make a plan for my future. Tonight as I lay down in my bedroom, I started thinking about love. The sun is going down and the time of the owl is beginning.

It's incredible what I can do now that I am not a slave to drugs, that took my full attention everyday. Any hope I had for a career was shot, any idea of a bright future was so lost before and now I have it in my hands again. It's a miraculous feeling. When I reflect on love now, being in a sober and healthy mind, I can feel my romantic side finally blooming again. Love is simple or so it should be. I have been in every sort of abusive relationship possible and I have met all different types of love. I won't settle for anything less than what I know I deserve.

The morning comes and it's incredible being sober and not hungover while having no desire to get drugs. In my next relationship I will be heard, and my heart will be properly handled with love, proper love. It makes me sad when I think of the people I have been in love with. I don't think it's their fault that they don't know what love actually looks like. It's learned behavior. People don't come out evil. If they don't have a proper role model, parents, that either lead by example or at least teach them what love is and how they should show love then they know no difference. I can have empathy and compassion for those people however I will no longer be a punching bag for them nor will I hold their bleeding baggage. I will love how I have never been loved before.

I found myself going through all my photos that I have stored on my one drive, on my computer that I have kept during my addiction. All the men, the schemes, the screenshots and so much more. I find myself thinking a lot about Jason and me. We have lots of photos of us during our addiction. When I start to remember the good, the bad comes shortly behind that.

After I closed my computer tonight, I feel like I know what I need to do. He calls me from the recovery house ,he is at daily right now and he says he loves me but I just don't feel the same. Everytime I think of ending it with him though I find myself getting sad. I want to trust him again but there is just so much baggage. He is wanting to make plans and move back in with each other, but I just don't feel confident enough with the connection we now have. It's still new. I know what love is and what it looks like, I know what I offer as a partner to another human and I don't think he can give me what I truly deserve.

I won't let what happened between Jason and me affect my ability to love again. Just because my love was treated horribly doesn't give me a right to continue the pattern. I could, but that would be counterproductive for what my goal is in obtaining that great love I know I desire. A person who is having their love abused, like I did, I find myself wondering who needs the counsel more, me or them. As much as I need to be warned that love can be used as a tool to be manipulated by, the person doing it to me also needs imperative education just as much. I can now look with pity upon them because they didn't have a role model to truly show them how to love..

They have no idea what unconditional love feels like or how it can make them feel, some of the most powerful human emotions this world has to offer us. They have been robbed which is why they now do the robbing. As I have said before, hurt people... hurt people.

They say, you attract what you are, but in certain environments around certain people I found that isn't the case. If I am a sheep among wolves, I am not going to attract sheep and I certainly will get the attention of a wolf in this circumstance. I needed to remove myself from the wolves and start living among other sheep to have a beautiful future.

Some people prey on people like me and take advantage of how I am wired. I think the more important lesson that I have learned is where I choose to exist and who I choose to exist around is key. I have tasted every flavor of love and I have seen every dynamic possible. I have been the abuser, to a degree, and the abused. I have been the woman and I have been the man in different relationships. I have tried every sexuality, being the dominant or perfect submissive. I have learned that no matter what position I held with a person, it all comes down to the fact that we are just people.

We are people and there is a certain chemistry and attraction that we all look for and find ourselves drawn to. True innocent love is blind and if my mind and heart is open enough I found that love didn't discriminate nor did it care about gender. No matter what, it shouldn't be used for personal advantage or gain. It shouldn't have conditions or rules and most certainly shouldn't be complicated. Complicated? I hate that category on facebook, if it's complicated then uncomplicate it. Usually that just means that the person is scared to face the reality of their situation with someone and ignorance is bliss.

I think about the visions while I have been in my deepest despair of the world and how it truly revolves. I could get lost in all the horror I have been through or I could keep in mind that I am on a giant rock floating in the middle of the universe in the middle of nowhere and it could end at any time. We are all here for the human experience, I need to make the most of it. I am wiser now with all of my discoveries and have lived so many different lives, some that many won't ever live or make it out alive.

As I wipe my tears, I begin to think about some of the darkness I went through. I literally have to tell myself to focus and really dig into my mind and bring myself back to those really dark moments to write about them. Even if the world has darkness, I could either submit to that or be a bright light in the middle of darkness because those that don't have a voice or are stuck in someone else's mind game like I was….. I will be their muse.

So many people get stuck especially when they don't have support, but if they want it enough, they can find support in places they never thought of looking. YOU are all YOU need. What I have learned is I could have all the support and money with resources in the world but if I am not ready or willing, none if it matters. As I start to close my eyes, one permanent thought perpetrates my mind… I can break the pattern or the pattern will break me. Everything had to come from within myself to believe and really apply my efforts to make a change and finally search for the life I lost.

Recovery is a journey, not a destination. It's a path that requires patience, self-compassion, and an unwavering commitment to healing. When I first entered sobriety, I was terrified. Terrified of facing my demons, terrified of confronting the trauma I had buried for so long. But I knew I had no other choice- I had to face the darkness if I ever wanted to find the light.

The early days of recovery were some of the hardest of my life. I was stripped raw, forced to confront the pain I had spent years avoiding. But as I worked through the trauma, layer by layer, something incredible began to happen. The hold that addiction had over me started to loosen, and in its place, I found a glimmer of hope- a hope that maybe I could rebuild myself and my life. Writing became a lifeline, a place where I could finally unpack the trauma that had fueled my addiction. I began to understand that my substance abuse was never about the drug, it was about the deep-seated wounds that I had never allowed to heal. With each painful memory I unearthed, I felt a little lighter, a little closer to the person I wanted to be.

Recovery is not a straight line. There are setbacks, relapses, moments of doubt. But with each step forward, I learned to trust myself again, to believe that I was worthy of a life free from the chains of addiction. I surrounded myself with people who supported my journey, who believed in my ability to heal even when I couldn't see it for myself.

As the fog of addiction lifted, I began to rediscover the parts of myself that had been lost. I reconnected with my passions, my dreams, and the people I had pushed away. I learned to forgive myself for the mistakes I had made, to let go of the shame that had held me captive for so long.

Today, I stand on the other side of addiction, a survivor of both trauma and substance abuse. My journey hasn't been easy, and there are still days when the darkness creeps in, when the scars of the past feel fresh and raw. But I've learned that I am stronger than I ever imagined, that I have the power to create a life filled with love, purpose and meaning.

My story is a testament to that journey- a journey from *the fall to addiction & rise to recovery*. It's a story of pain, but also of resilience, of the human spirit's incredible capacity to heal and grow. It's a reminder that no matter how far you've fallen, it's never too late to rise, to reclaim your life, and to find the light within the shadows.

There is a reason we addicts choose to turn to, and believe in God…It is because we have met, and danced with, the devil…

EPILOGUE

As I close this chapter of my life, I want to extend a heartfelt message to anyone who may be struggling with addiction or recovery. My journey through the depths of despair in addiction and the rise to sobriety has shown me that hope is always within reach, no matter how dark the path may seem. Recovery is not just possible; it is a journey filled with growth, resilience, and transformation. If you find yourself feeling lost or hopeless, please know that you are not alone. There is help available, and reaching out can be the first step toward a brighter future. Whether you are seeking support through a professional or a peer, I encourage you to take that brave step. As a certified professional peer support worker, I am here to offer my assistance in any way I can. Remember, you past does not define you; it is merely a part of your story. Embrace the possibility of change and the promise of recovery. Do not give up on yourself. The journey may be challenging, but is also incredibly rewarding. Together, we can find our way to a life worth living. You can do this. It is never to late. For those still in active addiction, a life full of drugs and crime truly only has two endings. Either death or jail. There is no other climax. If you have a will, you will find a way.

Printed in Great Britain
by Amazon